TWENTIETH CENTURY
# INTERPRETATIONS

MAYNARD MACK, *Series Editor*
Yale University

NOW AVAILABLE
*Collections of Critical Essays*
ON

TWENTIETH CENTURY INTERPRETATIONS
OF

# UTOPIA

TWENTIETH CENTURY INTERPRETATIONS
OF

# U T O P I A

*A Collection of Critical Essays*

Edited by
WILLIAM NELSON

Prentice-Hall, Inc.  *Englewood Cliffs, N. J.*

A SPECTRUM BOOK

93073

Current printing (last number):
10   9   8   7   6   5   4   3   2   1

# Contents

# Introduction

## by William Nelson

There are villages named "Utopia" in Texas and Kansas. New Brunswick has a Lake Utopia and New York City a Utopia Parkway. It is an odd place name, for the Greek roots of the word mean "No Place."

The author of the book that made No Place famous was Thomas More (1477 or 1478–1535), son of a prosperous London lawyer and judge. In a fashion then not uncommon for children of the gentry, the young More was placed in the household of Archbishop (later Cardinal) Morton, Lord Chancellor of the realm under Henry VII, to serve as page, learn his letters and his manners, and listen to the conversation of the great. At about the age of thirteen or fourteen he went to Oxford where he spent some two years, though at which college or college grammar school is uncertain. Humanist enthusiasm for classical studies had begun to take hold in England at this time and the boy was touched by it: the biography written by his son-in-law William Roper says that at Oxford "he was both in the Greek and Latin tongue sufficiently instructed." But he was destined for the law, and by 1496 he had progressed far enough in that discipline to be admitted to Lincoln's Inn, one of the Inns of Court, the professional associations and schools for civil jurisprudence in England. He did not abandon his literary interests, however. In 1499 he met Erasmus, who was to become his life-long friend, and escorted him on a visit to the schoolroom in which the king's children (including young Henry) were being taught by the poet John Skelton. And two years later he wrote to a schoolmaster friend, "You will ask me how I am getting on with my studies. Excellently; nothing could be better. I am giving up Latin, and taking to Greek."

We have only scraps of information about More's career during the first decade of the sixteenth century and they present no very coherent picture. He is said to have been a member of parliament who earned the king's displeasure by opposing a request for a special subsidy. He practiced law in collaboration with his father. He lectured to a London audience on the historical aspects of St. Augustine's *City of God*. Roper tells us that he thought of entering a religious order and spent some time, perhaps several years, in a house of the Carthusians. He tormented himself by wearing a hair shirt. In 1505 he married Jane Colt, a girl of seventeen, who bore him four children, Margaret, Elizabeth, Cecily, and John. According to Erasmus he wrote a defense of Plato's proposal (in the *Republic*) that wives be held communally, no doubt as a joke or a rhetorical exercise. In company with William Lily, later master of the famous school of St. Paul's, he translated Greek epigrams into Latin, and he composed some Latin ones of his own. With Erasmus he translated into Latin a number of the dialogues of Lucian, the second century Greek satirist. He wrote some inconsiderable English verse and translated into English a biography of Pico della Mirandola, Italian humanist philosopher. When Henry VIII came to the throne in 1509, More presented him with a Latin poem of conventionally fulsome praise, elegantly inscribed and illuminated on vellum.

He became increasingly involved in civic affairs. The powerful guild of Mercers employed him in negotiations with the merchants of the Low Countries, negotiations that required both his legal training and his skill as a Latin orator, and rewarded him with the valuable privilege of guild membership. In 1510 he was appointed one of the undersheriffs of the city, a legal office that Erasmus tells us was a very honorable one, though requiring little work. Roper's testimony is similar: "By which office and his learning together, as I have heard him say, he gained without grief not so little as four hundred pounds by the year." An income of that size must have made More a very rich man.

His business affairs did not keep him from writing. Probably in 1514 he wrote his first major work, a history of the usurpation of the throne by Richard III. He composed both a Latin version and an English one. The style is lively and dramatic; strongly influenced by such classical historians as Sallust and Livy, the book is an early example of humanist historiography in England and the first in English. The portrait of a villainous Richard that More painted determined attitudes toward that king for centuries. The English version was quoted whole by Holinshed and other historians of the sixteenth century, and Shakespeare borrowed freely from it, both matter and phrase, for his play on the subject. To what extent More's portrait is a deliberate distortion is a question that has been much debated. Certainly, despite an appearance of objectivity, More did not hesitate to retail such rumors ("It is for truth reported . . .") as that Richard was born "not untoothed," evidence of his "unnatural" character.

The year 1515 marks a decided turn in More's career. Negotiations concerning the wool trade and other matters required the dispatch of an embassy to the Low Countries, and in May, at the request of the London merchants, More was made a member of the government mission. He spent the next six months in Bruges and Antwerp. At some time during his stay at Bruges the fiction of *Utopia* records the meeting of More, his "pupil-servant" John Clement, and a friend, Peter Giles, scholar and town clerk of Antwerp, with the wise, weather-beaten traveler to distant lands, Raphael Hythloday. In More's garden, seated on a bench covered with grass turf, Hythloday recounted to More and his companions his strange experiences in the New World and in the island of Utopia. Of course, there is no reason to suppose that any such conversation actually took place, with or without the mysterious traveler: the fictional dialogue in which the interlocutors included real people (like Giles and Clement) was a favorite genre among Renaissance humanists.

It was during his stay in the Low Countries or soon after his return to England that More wrote the work by which he is principally known. The description of the island of Utopia, which constitutes Book II, was written first, probably with an introduction corresponding to the first pages of Book I as we have it. The remainder of Book I, in which the question is debated as to whether Hythloday should seek to enter royal service and the discussion turns to the ills of contemporary Europe, appears to have been an afterthought. In September, 1516, More sent the manuscript to Erasmus with the request that he solicit for it letters of recommendation by scholars and statesmen. The first edition of this Latin text, printed at Louvain, appeared in time for copies to be presented in January, 1517. Other editions appeared in succeeding years. The first English translation was made long after More's death by Ralph Robynson in 1551.

The debate in Book I of *Utopia* as to whether the entrance of a wise man into royal service would result in benefit to the commonwealth or corruption of the counselor perhaps reflects a personal indecision. After More's return from the Low Countries, the King offered him a pension that he refused, fearing a conflict of interest with his responsibilities to the city. But a year or so later he did accept membership in the royal council, or was dragged into it as Erasmus says, and he broke his official connection with the city by resigning his office of under-sheriff. In 1521 he was knighted; in 1523 he served as Speaker of Parliament; in 1529, after the fall of Wolsey, he was made Lord Chancellor.

More's legal knowledge and his association with the London merchants undoubtedly contributed to his usefulness to the crown, but his duties as servant to the King and to Wolsey seem principally to have required his talents as persuasive orator, diplomat, and writer of official letters. His skill as an orator came to public notice in the year of his entry into royal service, 1517. On what came to be known as Evil May Day of that year, the London apprentices broke into a violent riot directed against the foreign artisans in the city. At the request of the Privy Council More harangued the mob, and his eloquence "almost brought them to a stay" though a fresh incident roused their fury again. In succeeding years he served in diplomatic negotiations with the merchants of the Hanseatic League, helped to arrange a meeting between Henry and the Emperor Charles V, attended the meeting between Henry and Francis I of France. Roper remarks that whenever the King visited Oxford or Cambridge he would always assign More the task of responding extempore to the eloquent orations which greeted him. Among More's extensive official correspondence is a letter by which he intervened in the King's name in support of those Oxford scholars enthusiastic for the new study of Greek who were being harassed by their conservative colleagues. He served as "sorter out and placer of the principal matters" for the King's Latin pamphlet attacking Luther, *The Assertion of the Seven Sacraments*. As Speaker, in 1523, he urged Commons to grant a large subsidy to pay for war in France, and in 1529, now as Chancellor of the realm, he addressed that body again in a bitter attack upon his fallen predecessor and former superior, Thomas Wolsey.

There is no sign that More's presence on the royal council brought England any closer to a utopian state. He may have argued privately against costly and unnecessary wars, but Henry, like the French king satirized in the first book of *Utopia*, continued to follow his impossible dreams of regaining his "inheritance" of France. No doubt Hythloday was right when he said that in the deliberations of the great the counsel of the wise would only be laughed at.

His home was easier to control. Erasmus described it as a Christian version of Plato's Academy. About 1525 the family moved from London to a large house in suburban Chelsea. The establishment was presided over by More's second wife, Alice, whom he had married a month after the death of his first wife in 1511. She was, More said, "nec bella nec puella"—"neither a pearl nor a girl" as R. W. Chambers translates it. However devoted she was to her husband she could make no sense either of his interest in learning or of his insistence upon principle which led to his martyrdom. But the children were educated by private tutors along proper humanist lines: the classical languages, history, philosophy, astronomy, studies in which the oldest daughter Margaret proved to be by far the most talented. Nightly prayer and Bible-reading at mealtime were regular institutions. For amusement and relaxation More kept a fool and the monkey who appears in Holbein's drawing of the family group, but, as in Utopia, dice and card-playing were forbidden.

Had More become Chancellor earlier than 1529 he might have been able to put into practice some of the ideas suggested by Hythloday in

Book I of *Utopia*. But the opportunity was gone. The principal pre-occupations now were the great religious schism and the King's "matter," the annulment of the marriage to Catherine of Aragon, problems originally quite separate but soon to grow together. On both heads More's position was probably known to the King before he was elevated to the chancellorship. Nevertheless, his convictions led to his resignation of that post three years later, and two years after that to his execution.

During his chancellorship, More took an active part in the suppression of what he and the church hierarchy considered heresy. Religious persecution suddenly became more frequent and rigorous, and during the last six months of his tenure of the office three or more heretics were burnt alive. More was present at some of the trials. His responsibility for these executions and for other cases in which the victims were flogged or imprisoned without trial has been much debated. His defenders point out that condemnation for heresy was the judgment of the clergy, not of the lay, and that the state merely carried out the sentences on the ground that an excommunicated heretic endangered its security. To those who charge More with inconsistency because his Utopians permit not only freedom of religious belief but also the right of rational persuasion to all who accept the idea of God and of afterlife, they reply that the Utopians lack revelation of the true faith and the situations are therefore not comparable. Furthermore, it is argued, the Utopians themselves harshly punish those who aggressively try to convert people to their beliefs and disparage the faith of others, so breaching the peace. Yet the sense of inconsistency remains. It is difficult to believe that the ecclesiastical authorities of Tudor times acted without regard to the opinion of the chief officer of the realm, there present in the court. Nor is it recorded in More's fiction that the Utopians burnt criminals of whatever kind.

More's efforts to suppress heretical beliefs were not limited to his official role. During the years of his service on the royal council he had written little on his own except for a devout treatise which he left unfinished entitled *The Four Last Things*—the four things every man should think about constantly: death, judgment, heaven, and hell. Now the church hierarchy urged him to employ his eloquence in the confutation of "pernicious" ideas, which had become increasingly widespread. More responded with a long treatise in English entitled *A Dialogue of Sir Thomas More of Images, Praying to Saints, Other Things Touching the Pestilent Sect of Luther and Tyndale*. The *Dialogue* imagines that a nameless friend had been hearing strange notions about religion and to satisfy the doubts that had arisen sent a messenger to More to pose the questions to him. In the garden (More evidently loved gardens) and at dinner, More and the

messenger converse amicably and rationally. The result is the destruction of heretical arguments, to be sure, but despite the word
"pestilent" of the title the tone is not as immoderate or uncivilized
as in the pamphlets that followed. For the *Dialogue* produced Tyndale's *Answer* and that in turn More's *Confutation* of the answer.
So arose a general propaganda war characterized on both sides by
increasing anger, intolerance, and brutality.

More's literary campaign against heresy carried over beyond his
resignation of the Great Seal in 1532. By that time the urgency of the
King's desire for annulment of his marriage to Catherine, which More
could not in conscience approve, rendered his position untenable.
Bad health provided the excuse.

In 1534 the blow which More had surely long expected fell at last.
He was arrested as a traitor, a loose and accommodating term in those
days. There were, to be sure, other charges laid against him, but the
nub of the matter was his refusal to sign an oath in support of the Act
of Supremacy, which made the king head of the church in England
and so allowed that English church to make final judgment on the
royal divorce. To prove the charge of treason it was necessary to show
that the accused had not merely in thought but also by words or
writing denied the king his supremacy, and evidence, perhaps falsified,
was brought forth to prove that More had done so. But the trial merely
confirmed Henry's decision: with the legitimacy of the children he
expected by Anne Boleyn at stake it would not do to permit the
legality of his marriage to remain uncertain. A former Lord Chancellor, well known to the élite of Europe, who refused to affirm the
grounds of that legality constituted a living challenge to it.

While in prison More wrote his last book, the *Dialogue of Comfort
against Tribulation*. As its title suggests, it is in the tradition of prison
literature made famous by the *Consolations of Philosophy* written
by Boethius in the fifth century as he awaited execution by the Emperor Theodoric. But More's book is really a rejection of Boethius,
for at the very beginning he insists that no philosophy can suffice to
console the troubled man; his only hope rests on his faith in Christ's
promise of redemption.

King Henry was gracious enough in this case to mitigate the sentence of hanging, drawing, and quartering to a simple beheading.
On July 6, 1535, the sentence was executed. More's adopted daughter
Margaret, wife of that John Clement who listened to Hythloday's
account of Utopia, was present. She reports that he begged the by-
standers "earnestly to pray for the King, that it might please God to
give him good counsel, protesting that he died the King's good servant
but God's first."

The recorded events of a man's life can scarcely suggest the im-

pression he left upon his contemporaries, and this is surely the case
with Thomas More. Erasmus has given us a description of his friend
in a letter he wrote to a German humanist. He emphasizes More's
kindliness and generosity, his gift for friendship, his unimpeachable
honesty, his lack of ambition and disregard for formalities, the mod-
esty of his habits, his unfailing cheerfulness, his love of a jest. Others
who had the opportunity of knowing him, like the Spanish scholar
Ludovico Vives, testify to the same traits. A grammarian of the period
set the following passage for his students to translate into Latin:

> More is a man of an angel's wit and singular learning. He is a man of
> many excellent virtues; if I should say as it is, I know not his fellow.
> For where is the man in whom is so many goodly virtues of that gentle-
> ness, lowliness, and affability? And as time requireth, a man of marvelous
> mirth and pastimes, and sometimes of as sad [i.e., sober] gravity. As who
> say, a man for all seasons.

William Roper wrote the biography of his father-in-law long after
his death, about the time of the accession of Elizabeth in 1558. The
book is less an account of More's life than an attempt to portray his
character, for it is filled with anecdotes illustrating his wisdom, his
foresight, and his saintliness—that is, his imitation of the life of
Christ. Other members of the group of Roman Catholic exiles during
the reign of Elizabeth wrote similar books elaborating on Roper's
story and emphasizing More's claim to canonization. From the Protestant controversialists of More's day and after, of course, a different
picture emerges: his wit becomes frivolity and tergiversation, the firm-
ness of his faith becomes intolerance and cruelty. But even among his
Protestant enemies a note of regret is sometimes sounded—what a pity
that so learned and witty a man should have been so misled! And
during Elizabeth's reign a group of dramatists, one of whom may
well have been Shakespeare, wrote a play on the subject of More's
life giving full weight to those qualities recorded by Erasmus and
others and concluding with the judgment,

> A very learned worthy gentleman
> Seals error with his blood.

*Utopia* was the product of More's happier years, before he became
involved in the affairs of government and disastrous conflicts. It came
as the culmination of a literary rather than a political career, after
More had exercised himself in such typically humanist activities as
the writing of Latin epigrams, translation from the Greek, and historiography. To be sure, the humanists believed that their knowledge
of the history and moral philosophy of the ancients and their mastery
of the art of persuasion fitted them peculiarly to be counselors to

kingdoms, and More evidently shared that view. Much of what is
said in both books of *Utopia* is comment on and reaction to the
political, social, and economic scene of the day. But the form and
feature, if not the substance, of *Utopia* was determined by the literary
traditions out of which it grew.

When the Utopian traveler Raphael Hythloday is described at the
beginning of the book he is compared with Plato and Ulysses, a comparison that serves neatly to define the principal roots of More's work:
the imagination of a "best state of a commonwealth" and the report
of a wise traveler to strange lands. Plato's *Republic* is the type of the
former, and its inspiration for More is obvious if only from his adoption of its system of communal ownership for his Utopia, though it
should be noted that Plato's communism is for the élite only, whereas
More's is general. He must also have been familiar with philosophic
discussions of the ideal state by Aristotle, Cicero, and Seneca, and the
pseudohistorical account in Plutarch. But Utopia, in More's fiction,
is not a logical construct like Plato's but a real island located in a
real sea, and the report of it is a traveler's tale. The *Odyssey* itself, and
a variety of stories of fabulous voyages in ancient times and in the
Middle Ages, provided the models for such a discourse. In fact, like
Lucian (a great favorite of both More and Erasmus), More makes fun
of the tradition at the same time as he makes use of it: his is to be a
philosophical voyage, one in search not of marvelous monsters but of
a greater wonder than these, a community of well and wisely trained
citizens. And in addition to the library of fabulous and burlesque
voyages there had recently appeared the circumstantial account of the
expeditions of Amerigo Vespucci to the new-found lands. More's story
makes Hythloday a member of the fourth of those voyages. But though
More may have borrowed a few details from the explorer's description
of the tribes he had encountered he shows no real interest in the nature
of those peoples or in the possibilities created by the discoveries. For
the purposes of *Utopia,* Vespucci's narrative was merely a conveniently
contemporary traveler's tale.

The combination of Platonic and Odyssean strains creates a tone
that is at once the charm of the work and the despair of its inter-
preters. The seriousness of the criticism of European ways and of the
plea for enlightened rationality cannot be questioned. Nor can the
jocularity of the choice of names (Hythloday means "talker of nonsense"; Ademus, "king without people"; Anyder, "waterless river,"
and so on), the mock precision of the argument about the length of
the bridge at Amaurote, and the extravagance and absurdity of some
Utopian customs. There is the upside-down device, too, for the wonderful island is located rather vaguely in the antipodes, its shape is
roughly circular as England's is roughly triangular, its people use gold

for chamber pots and as shackles for prisoners. The combination of jest and earnest was, of course, no invention of More's though it was consonant with his habit of telling jokes with a straight face; in both ancient and medieval times the seriocomic mode was perhaps more common than it is today. A few years before More wrote the *Utopia,* Erasmus dedicated to him his *Praise of Folly* (or rather *Folly's Speech in Praise of Herself*), an oration in which foolishness, mockery, and grave wisdom are inextricably entwined. For this work, too, disentangling jest from earnest has proved very difficult for modern readers.

As a result, interpretations of *Utopia* range from the acceptance of the island's constitution not only as a desirable ideal but even as a political program, an end that men might achieve, to a characterization of the book as an amusingly ingenious fantasy or an ironical presentation of ideas More heartily disliked. The problem of deciding when More means what he says and when he does not is further complicated by his adoption of the method of dialogue, for it is not clear whether he speaks through the character to whom he gives his own name, through his fiction of the wise Hythloday, or neither. And the character "More" himself does not always speak with one voice. Toward the end of Book I he makes a rational defense of private property on the ground that it provides the stimulus essential to the orderly production of goods, but at the end of Book II the same "More" attacks private property by offering the transparently specious defense that distinctions of wealth are the sole basis of nobility, magnificence, worship, honor, and majesty, "as the common opinion is."

Inevitably, commentators have endeavored to reconcile what seem to be More's attitudes in *Utopia* with his later writings and actions. The apparent disparity between Utopian religious tolerance and the Lord Chancellor's rigor has already been touched upon. But how to account for such Utopian institutions as euthanasia and divorce, both forbidden by the Church for which More died? Or for tactics like subornation of treason, assassination of enemy rulers, and forcible annexation of foreign lands the natural resources of which, in Utopian judgment, have been insufficiently exploited? The most inclusive explanation, apart from the dismissal of *Utopia* as a *jeu d'esprit* or an ironical encomium, depends upon the fact that the Utopians are conceived of as deprived of the revelation of Christianity, so that they must depend for guidance only upon their reason and their "natural" religion. Their ordinances are therefore to be taken not as a prescription for European nations to follow but as a sharp criticism of the irrationality of those nations, a demonstration of what human reason, even without the aid of the true faith, is capable of achieving. As for euthanasia and divorce, defenders of More's consistency point out that in Utopia these practices are hedged about with so many restrictions that they are in effect almost nullified. Utopian foreign policy and military tactics, it is argued, are consonant with the law of nature, if not of Christ. The Utopians, after all, fight for what they consider a true good and try to win their wars with as little bloodshed as possible unlike Christian Europeans who fight on the pretense of honor and set royal prestige above the lives and welfare of the commons.

The variety of modern interpretations of *Utopia* echoes the variety of comments on the work made by More's contemporaries, members of the humanist circle of northern Europe. Some applaud its "festivity," others remark on the lessons it teaches against greed and hypocrisy, one expresses the hope that Europe adopt the Utopian constitution, another proclaims it a vision of a kind of paradise lower than heaven itself but far above the world we know. What Henry VIII or other European monarchs or their chief ministers thought of it, if they read it at all, we have no way of telling.

Some fifteen years after the publication of *Utopia,* François Rabelais made Gargantua a citizen of that fortunate country. Like More, Rabelais mingles jest and earnest, describes strange lands with remarkable customs, and devises a community dedicated to the rational pursuit of happiness. He does these things in his own way, to be sure, and it is a very different way from More's, yet, in the opinion of the great modern scholar Erich Auerbach, Rabelais owed more to More than to any other of his contemporaries.

From Renaissance times onward, the *Utopia* has been the inspiration for innumerable imaginary voyages to countries with institutions and customs differing radically from those we know. The voyages may be to distant lands, to planets, to the dim past or into the future. The country visited may indeed be the author's conception of an ideal state, or it may represent what he expects or fears will be the world of the future, or it may reflect our world in caricature or upside down. What most of these fictions have in common is their establishment of a viewpoint outside of our everyday environment from which we can look at ourselves objectively, with fresh eyes. Essentially, therefore, Utopian voyages turn inward rather than outward; they do not escape from this world but concern themselves with it.

That More so understood his own fiction is evident from his decision to add the dialogue of Book I to the account of the Utopian commonwealth which he had first composed. In this part of the work the wisdom and experience of the far-traveled Hythloday are brought to bear upon the ills and confusions of contemporary Europe and England in particular. The result is a questioning of long-established ways and opinions. Is severe punishment the best way of preventing crime? What is gained when a nation enlarges its territories? Is it healthy for a realm to maintain a standing army? Should landowners be permitted to use their land as they see fit? Can a philosopher really be of service to a king? Modern historians have questioned the validity of some aspects of More's analysis of England's economic state and doubted the effectiveness of the remedies he proposed. But the value of the discussion in Book I rests upon the freshness of its approach, its search for causes, its proposal of new ways of dealing with old problems.

However original and penetrating the dialogue of Book I of the *Utopia* may be, it is the description of the island and its constitution in Book II that has given the name Utopia to a variety of localities and the word "utopian" the status of a common adjective. Underlying such usage is the assumption that More had intended to describe an ideal community or one as nearly ideal as humanity permits. For centuries some men, at least, have entertained the hope that radical and lasting solutions to human ills may indeed be found, whether by starting afresh in some uninhabited place or by violent uprooting of the old, sick world. Their conceptions of what the hoped-for community should be differ widely; they may be inspired by religion or philosophy or economic theory. These conceptions they identify with Utopia, not in terms of its specific ordinances, but rather in what they take to be its aspiration for a brave new world. Yet "Utopia" is after all No Place, so that when a plan is described as "utopian," the mocker expresses his belief that ultimate solutions of the problems of this world are mere dreams, incapable of realization. Shakespeare's *The Tempest* (II, i, 144ff.) offers us both the dreamer and his mockers. Gonzalo proposes to create a new commonwealth to excel the Golden Age, a commonwealth in which all things are executed "by contraries." His companions ridicule him and Alonso, King of Naples, puts an end to the discussion with "Prithee, no more; thou dost talk nothing to me." Whether or not Shakespeare remembered that the name Hythloday meant "talker of nonsense," his Gonzalo and Alonso are both of the spirit of More's *Utopia*.

## PART ONE

*Interpretations*

# Utopian Socialism

## *by Karl Kautsky*

After More has given in detail the picture of an ideal society which forms the exact opposite of the society of his time, at the conclusion of *Utopia* he once more flings down the gauntlet in a vehement apostrophe. Modern Socialism has hardly emitted a sharper criticism of society than is contained in the sentences with which Hythloday concludes his account of the Utopians.

\* \* \*

Compared with this bold criticism, which attacks society at its roots, how limited does not the much belauded action of Luther appear, who commenced a year after the appearance of *Utopia* to preach against, not indulgences themselves, but the abuse of indulgences, and was impelled to take further steps not by a logical process going on in his mind, but by the logic of facts! And yet while the whole might of Rome was eventually summoned against the man who attacked the abuse of indulgences, without purposing to make any change in the ecclesiastical organization, no molestation was offered to the man whose doctrines tended to sap the very foundations of society; and the advocate of a church which was as uncatholic, and in many respects even unchristian, as any one of the reformed churches, became a martyr of the Catholic religion.

Strange as this difference in treatment appears, there was good reason for it. Luther addressed himself to the masses; he expressed the interests of powerful classes and parties. More, with his aspirations, stood alone; he addressed only a small circle of scholars, the people did not understand him and he did not desire to be understood by the people. He therefore wrote his *Utopia* in Latin, and concealed his thoughts in the garment of satire, which to be sure permitted him greater freedom in the expression of his opinions.

This brings us to the last question which remains to be answered: What did More aim at in his *Utopia*?

We know that some regard it merely as an imitation of the Platonic Republic, while others declare it to be an idle fantasy.

We believe, however, that we have sufficiently shown that More's communism differs essentially from that of Plato, and instead of being "a splendid fruit of the study of antiquity," as Rudhart would have us believe in his *Thomas Morus,* it is the product of the social evils and incipient economic tendencies of the Renascence; and that it is based on living actualities, and not on antiquarian book wisdom.

The idea that it was written as a jest may be dismissed. It was taken very seriously by More's contemporaries. Budæus, for example, wrote to Lupsetus: "We are greatly indebted to Thomas More for his *Utopia,* in which he holds up to the world a model of social felicity. Our age and our posterity will regard this exposition as a source of excellent doctrines and useful ordinances, from which States will construct their institutions." Numerous other contemporaries of More express themselves in a similar sense, scholars and statesmen like Johannes Paludanus, Paulus Jovius and Hieronymus Buslidianus. Stapleton has collected a number of pronouncements upon *Utopia* all of which are couched in the terms of the above quotation. All saw in *Utopia* a book which gives directions to rulers how to govern their States.

And this was quite in accordance with the trend of that time. In the view then prevailing, everything was possible to a prince, and to those who gained the support of a prince. More's age was marked by a plethora of directions to princes. Machiavelli's *Prince* and Erasmus' *Manual for Christian Princes* were composed at the same time as *Utopia,* and we have not the slightest reason for doubting that the aim of the latter was the same as the aim of the former: to show princes how they should govern.

And *Utopia* even pursued the special object of influencing the government and constitution of England. This is not only shown very distinctly in the first book, but Erasmus, who ought to have known it, relates this fact in his well-known letter to Hutten: "He published his *Utopia* for the purpose of showing, what are the things that occasion mischief in commonwealths; having the English Constitution especially in view."

The island of Utopia is, in fact, England. More designed to show how England would look, and what shape her relations with abroad would assume, if she were communistically organized.

The analogy may be traced with exactitude: The island is separated from the Continent only by a channel 21 miles wide. The description of the capital, Amaurote, is a true description of London. Stow, in his *Survey of London,* finds a perfect correspondence between the two towns.

Historians and economists who are perplexed by *Utopia* perceive in this name a subtle hint by More that he himself regarded his communism as an impracticable dream.

In all the discussions about the Utopians there is only one element of a fantastic nature, and that is not the goal that was aimed at, but the ways and means of achieving it. More saw only one force which could carry communism into effect, and this he mistrusted. He has shown us in his *Utopia* in what manner he conceived that communism would be enforced. A prince named Utopus conquered the country, and impressed on it the stamp of his mind; all institutions in Utopia are to be traced to him. He thought out the general plan of the commonwealth and then put it into execution.

In this way More conceived the realization of his ideals: he was the father of Utopian Socialism, which was rightly named after his *Utopia.* The latter is utopian less on account of the impracticability of its aims than on account of the inadequacy of the means at its disposal for their achievement.

We know that More could not help being an Utopist. As yet there was no party, no class to champion Socialism; the decisive political power, on which the State seemed to depend, were the princes, then a young, and in a sense a revolutionary element, without defined traditions: why should not one of them be converted to communism? If such a prince desired, he could enforce communism. If no prince so desired, the poverty of the people was unalterable. So thought More, and from this standpoint he was impelled to make an attempt to convert a prince. But he was by no means deceived as to the hopelessness of his task. He knew the princes of his time too well.

He concludes *Utopia* with the following words, after inserting a saving clause that he did not agree with all that Hythloday had related: "However, there are many things in the commonwealth of Utopia that I rather wish, than hope, to see followed in our governments."

In this conclusion lies the whole tragedy of More's fate, the whole tragedy of a genius who divines the problems of his age before the material conditions exist for their solution; the whole tragedy of a character who feels obliged to grapple with the solution of the problems which the age has presented, to champion the rights of the oppressed against the arrogance of the ruling classes, even when he stands alone and his efforts have no prospect of success.

More proved the grandeur of his character when he ascended the scaffold because he would not sacrifice his conviction to a princely caprice. It was already recognized by his contemporaries, who could not, however, grasp the magnitude of his genius, much as they praised it. Only in modern times, with the rise of scientific Socialism, has it become possible to do full justice to More the Socialist. Only since the second half of the nineteenth century have the aims of Socialism as a historic phenomenon been so obvious as to render it possible to separate the essential from the unessential, the permanent from the transitory in the beginnings of the Socialist Movement. Only with this has it become possible to perceive what in *Utopia* is the fantastic amusement of an idle hour, what is the echo of the past, what is a presentiment of the future, and what is historical fact.

And nothing speaks more eloquently for the greatness of the man, nothing shows more distinctly how he towered above his contemporaries, than that it required more than three centuries before the conditions existed which enable us to perceive that he set himself aims which are not the idle dreaming of a leisure hour, but the result of a profound insight into the essentials of the economic tendencies of his age. Although *Utopia* is more than four hundred years old, the ideals of More are not vanquished, but still lie before striving mankind.

# The Rational Heathens

## by R. W. Chambers

An ex-Cabinet minister is still alive who dates his political career from the accidental purchase of a copy of *Utopia* at a second-hand bookstall. One of his colleagues in the Cabinet has written of *Utopia,* that no treatise is better calculated to nourish the heart of a Radical. *Utopia* has become a textbook of Socialist propaganda. It did more to make William Morris a Socialist than ever Karl Marx did. All this testifies to its abiding power; yet we must never think of More as writing it for nineteenth-century Radicals or twentieth-century Socialists. Even he could not do that.

The first step to an appreciation of *Utopia* is to understand how it must have struck a scholar in the early sixteenth century. That is a difficult task, yet not an impossible one; and if we would understand More himself, it is a task which we must undertake.

We shall then find, I think, that few books have been more misunderstood than *Utopia*. It has given the English language a word "Utopian" to signify something visionary and unpractical. Yet the remarkable thing about *Utopia* is the extent to which it adumbrates social and political reforms which have either been actually carried into practice, or which have come to be regarded as very practical politics. Utopia is depicted as a sternly righteous and puritanical State, where few of us would feel quite happy; yet we go on using the word "Utopia" to signify an easy-going paradise, whose only fault is that it is too happy and ideal to be realized. *Utopia* is the first of a series which we have christened "Ideal Commonwealths." Some of these, for example William Morris' *News from Nowhere,* really *are* ideal. They are "Utopian" in the current sense, that is to say, they are quite unpractical fancies of what this world might be like if the dreamer could shatter it to bits, and then remold it nearer to the heart's desire. For instance, in *News from Nowhere* we might be sure that the Divine Worship of the citizens would be Morris' ideal. If he gives them

*From R. W. Chambers,* Thomas More *(London: Jonathan Cape, Ltd., 1935; New York: Harcourt, Brace & World, Inc., 1936), pp. 125–44. Reprinted by permission of Jonathan Cape, Ltd. and the Executors of the R. W. Chambers Estate.*

no Divine Worship, that also tells its tale. Now, More does not make his Utopians Christian. So modern scholars have argued: "Utopia is an ideal commonwealth; *argal* More thought the vague deism of his Utopians more ideal than the popular religious beliefs of his time."

Such argument might be reasonable if *Utopia* were a modern "Ideal Commonwealth." But we must never forget that More's education fell not in the nineteenth but in the fifteenth century. To a man educated in that century, the distinction was obvious between the virtues which might be taught by human reason alone, and the further virtues taught by Catholic orthodoxy. It was part of the medieval system to divide the virtues into the Four Cardinal Virtues (to which the heathen might attain) and the Three Christian Virtues. The Four Cardinal Virtues —Wisdom, Fortitude, Temperance, and Justice—are the foundation of Plato's commonwealths, as outlined in the *Republic* and the *Laws*.[1] These virtues were taken into the medieval system—part of the immense debt it owes to Greek philosophy. The Three Christian Virtues —Faith, Hope, and Charity—come of course from St. Paul's *First Epistle to the Corinthians*. Four and Three make Seven—the Perfect Number, which was extremely comforting. The perfect Christian character must comprise all seven. But the four heathen virtues were sufficient to ensure that a man or a State might be a model of conduct in secular matters. In Dante's *Divine Comedy* Virgil represents Philosophy, Reason, Human Wisdom. He is able to rescue Dante from the dark wood (although he was one of those who had not the three sacred virtues) because he knew and followed the four other virtues without fault. So Virgil can guide Dante till he meets Beatrice, but can go no further.

For a pattern of a State, Dante turns to Heathen Rome or to Heathen Greece. And it is not because of his deep learning that Dante does this. Our great English medieval poet, William Langland, the author of *Piers Plowman,* had but a commonplace education, but his system is similar. *Do Well* is the virtue of secular life, and the examples of it are the great non-Christian philosophers and rulers: Aristotle, Solomon, Socrates, Trajan. *Do Better* and *Do Best* represent forms of Christian virtues. And so More's friend, Busleiden, in his introductory letter to *Utopia,* tells us that the perfect commonwealth must unite "Wisdom in the ruler, Fortitude in the soldiers, Temperance in private individuals, and Justice in all."

In basing his *Utopia* upon these four heathen virtues, More is following medieval tradition; further, he is following his great examples, Plato's *Republic* and *Laws;* but, above all, he makes his satire upon contemporary European abuses more pointed. The virtues of

[1] *Republic,* Book IV; *Laws,* Book XII.

Heathen Utopia show up by contrast the vices of Christian Europe. But the Four Cardinal Virtues are subsidiary to, not a substitute for, the Christian Virtues. More has done his best to make this clear. It is not his fault if he has been misunderstood, as the following example will show.

Most of us would agree with Dame Alice in deploring More's extreme austerities. We have seen that, years before *Utopia* was written, she had complained to More's confessor about that shirt of hair. It was no good. It may have been some ten years after *Utopia* was written that, as Roper tells us, More's daughter-in-law, young Anne Cresacre, noticed it:

> My sister More, in the summer as he sat at supper, singly in his doublet and hose, wearing thereupon a plain shirt, without ruff or collar, chancing to spy, began to. laugh at it. My wife [Margaret Roper] not ignorant of his manner, perceiving the same, privily told him of it; and he, being sorry that she saw it, presently amended it. He used also sometimes to punish his body with whips, the cords knotted, which was known only to my wife, whom for her secrecy above all other he specially trusted, causing her, as need required, to wash the same shirt of hair.

Now, despite all this, we are told that the Utopians condemn bodily austerities as "a point of extreme madness, and a token of a man cruelly minded toward himself."

More's biographers and commentators have been puzzled. Yet the very next sentence of *Utopia* explains the puzzle. The Utopians have only reason to guide them, and they believe that *by man's reason* nothing can be found truer than their view, "*unless any godlier be inspired into man from Heaven.*" The same point is made by More later. There *are* orders of ascetics in *Utopia*: if the ascetics grounded their action on reason the Utopians would mock them; but as they base it on religion, the Utopians honor them and regard them as holy.

We find More, a dozen years later, urging against the Reformers this same doctrine which lies at the root of *Utopia:* "That Reason is servant to Faith, not enemy." More argues that Reason, Philosophy, and even Poetry have their part to play: zealots who, neglecting "a good mother wit" would cast away all learning except the Bible are, says More, "in a mad mind," and he quotes St. Jerome to prove that pagan Philosophy and Poetry have their use for Christians. By "Poetry" More of course means any work of the imagination: his Protestant critics decribe *Utopia* as "poetry," and More himself as a "poet." When a sixteenth-century Catholic depicts a pagan state founded on Reason and Philosophy, he is not depicting his ultimate ideal. Erasmus tells us that More's object was "to show whence spring the evils of States, with special reference to the English State, with which he was most familiar." The underlying thought of *Utopia* always is, *With nothing save Reason to guide them, the Utopians do this; and yet we Christian Englishmen, we Christian Europeans . . . !*

Just as More scored a point against the wickedness of Christian Europe, by making his philosophers heathen, so Jonathan Swift scored a point against the wickedness of mankind by representing *his* philosophers, the Houyhnhnms, as having the bodies of horses. Yet we do not call Swift inconsistent, because he did not live on a diet of oats, or, like poor Gulliver, fall into the voice and manner of horses in speaking. Swift did not mean that all horses are better than all men. He meant that some men are worse than horses. More did not mean that Heathendom is better than Christianity. He meant that some Christians are worse than heathen.

Dante and Langland and innumerable medieval writers had said the same before him. The conviction that life might be nobly lived on the basis of the four heathen cardinal virtues was one which the Catholic Middle Ages had inherited from Greek philosophy.

So, naturally, More is interested in the problem which for half a lifetime tormented Dante and Langland; what will be the fate, in the next world, of the just heathen, who are an example to us in the affairs of this world? More's answer is tentative, but he quotes with approval the "comfortable saying" of Master Nicholas de Lyra, the Franciscan, Dante's younger contemporary. Nicholas de Lyra argued that, though a much fuller faith is demanded from Christians, it suffices for the heathen to have believed "that God is, and that He is the rewarder of them that seek Him"; these are, says de Lyra, "two points such as every man may attain by natural reason, holpen forth with such grace as God keepeth from no man."

And More quoted this, not in his alleged "emancipated" youth, but in his last book, the *Treatise upon the Passion,* written in the Tower, when he had dismissed all wordly affairs, and was awaiting martyrdom "for the faith of the Catholic Church."

What, then, is the attitude of *Utopia* as to these two articles, which represent, in More's view, the orthodoxy to which a heathen may attain? King Utopus tolerated all varieties of belief and disbelief, save on these two points; he forbade, "earnestly and straitly" that any man should disbelieve in either (1) Divine Providence, or (2) a future life in which, as the Utopians believed, the just would be rewarded by God's presence.

So far was this simple creed from appearing lax to More's friends, that the marginal note (written either by Erasmus or by Peter Giles) contrasts the Utopian faith in immortality with the laxity and doubts of many Christians: *"The immortality of the soul, concerning which not a few, though Christians, to-day doubt or dispute."* But in Utopia, the man who disbelieves either of these articles is not counted as a citizen, or even as a man; he is excluded from all office, and despised, as being necessarily of a base and vile nature. To suffer lifelong public contumely, in a land where all life is lived in public, and where, save as a citizen, a man has and is nothing, is a punishment which many would feel to be worse than death. Yet the skeptic may not, publicly, argue in his own defense. Then comes the sentence which has been so often quoted, out of its context. In the old translation it runs, "How-beit they put him to no punishment." Of course, More did not write such nonsense. What he really says is, "They do not put him to any bodily punishment"—so long, that is, as he humbly submits to the disgrace and to the silence which his heresies involve. The charge against More of inconsistency rests upon refusing to notice his distinction between liberty to hold an opinion, and liberty to preach that opinion; between a man being in More's phrase "a heretic alone by himself," and being "a seditious heretic."

Bishop Creighton, to prove that More in later life "put his principles aside," quotes the passage which tells how King Utopus, when settling the Utopian constitution, found many religions prevalent in the land, and ordained that they should all be tolerated. Creighton then omits the passage about Utopus disgracing and muzzling those who held the opinions he thought pernicious. But this passage is vital; for, in the light of it, we find that Utopus did *not* tolerate the preaching of all views, but only of those which he, in his wisdom, thought tolerable. Then Creighton begins to quote again. Even those who held most noxious opinions "were put to no punishment." They are put to no bodily punishment, so long as they will submit to being disfranchised, despised, and silenced.

But, as the watchman says to Dogberry, "How if they will not?"

We can tell what would happen *then*, when we remember that, even in the discussion of such opinions as the State allows, any violent or seditious speech is punished in Utopia by banishment or bondage. And, in Utopia, if a man condemned to bondage jibs at his punishment, he is slain out of hand like a wild beast. Suppose that two skeptics, who did not believe the soul of man to be immortal, had discussed, in private, in Utopia, how they could get the law repealed which silenced and disfranchised them. They would have incurred the penalty imposed on those who plot against the fundamental laws of Utopia. And, even for the highest magistrates, that penalty is death.

Still, within these narrow limits, the Utopian has liberty of conscience. He may not spread among the common people a belief which the State thinks harmful, nor may he discuss the most innocent opinions in a way likely to cause sedition and dissension. He may not, in private, discuss any affair of State. But, if he submits to these restric-

tions, he is left alone; he is not to be terrorized into saying that he
believes what he does not believe.

It may be a low ideal of liberty which allows, to a man who holds
views disapproved by the authorities, freedom of thought only on condition that he does not claim freedom of speech. But that *is* the liberty
Utopia allows. . . .

But we merely confuse the issues if we use our modern, question-
begging terminology, and contrast More's alleged "emancipated youth"
with his orthodox old age. If we try to judge it in relation to the early
sixteenth century, we shall find that *Utopia* is by no means "emancipated"; it is rather a protest against undue "emancipation."

*Utopia* is, in part, a protest against the New Statesmanship: against
the new idea of the autocratic prince to whom everything is allowed.
I do not say that it is an impartial protest. The evil counsellors, who
are represented in the First Book of *Utopia* egging the prince to
despotism, might have replied that their ideal was not necessarily base
or sycophantic. Patriots have sometimes seen in tyranny the only
force strong enough to make their country great; reformers have
sometimes seen in it the only force strong enough to carry through the
reformation they desire. But *Utopia* is hostile to it.

Again, *Utopia* is, in part, a protest against the New Economics: the
enclosures of the great landowners, breaking down old law and custom,
destroying the old common-field agriculture. Here again, we must
not suppose that *Utopia* gives us the full story. There was much more
in the problem of enclosures than the greed of the great landlord, "the
very plague of his native country." The up-to-date farmer was also in
favor of sweeping away all traces of the older communal husbandry.
Thomas Tusser, a humble but practical agriculturist, says:

> Where all things in common do rest,
> Yet what doth it stand ye in stead?

Now, in contrast to this changing world, More depicts a state where
"all things in common do rest," and where there is no place for the
grabbing superman. More's theoretical *Utopia,* looking back to Plato's
*Republic* and to corporate life in the Middle Ages, probably seemed
to some contemporaries the reverse of "progressive." Cardinal Pole
has told of a conversation he had in his youth with Thomas Cromwell.
Cromwell ridiculed the *Republic* of Plato, which, after so many
centuries, had led to nothing. *He* had a book on statesmanship in
manuscript, by a practical modern writer, based on experience. The
book, which Cromwell offered to lend to Pole, was *The Prince* of
Nicholas Machiavelli.

It is noteworthy that the two most potent books on the State written
in the sixteenth century were written within so few years of each

other. Parts of *Utopia* read like a commentary on parts of *The Prince*, as Johnson's *Rasselas* reads like a commentary on Voltaire's *Candide*, though we know that in neither case can the English writer have read his continental predecessor. There is a reason for the coincidence; before *The Prince* was written, ideas used in *The Prince* had been gaining ground. They were the "progressive" ideas, and we may regard *Utopia* as a "reaction" against them. Over and over again, in Book I of *Utopia*, Raphael Hythloday imagines himself as counselling a prince, telling him what he ought to do, against those who are telling him what he *can* do; and always Raphael admits that these ideas of justice which he has brought from Utopia are opposed to all that the most up-to-date statesmen of Europe are thinking and doing.

And so, from the point of view of the new age of Machiavellian statesmanship and commercial exploitation, *Utopia* is old-fashioned. The King is to "live of his own," in medieval wise, and to turn a deaf ear to the counsellors who would make him all-powerful. The big landlords are to have mercy on their tenants, and not to allow them to be sacrificed to economic progress, and the law of supply and demand in the wool market.

And the outlook of *Utopia* on the ecclesiastical problems of 1516 is also conservative and orthodox. Among the most pressing problems of church government was that of the immunity of the clergy; among the most pressing problems of doctrine, the immortality of the soul; beyond all these was the problem of monasticism.

Most urgent in England, at this date, was the question of clerical immunity. If a cleric committed felony, was he to be hanged like a mere layman, or was he to be left to the gentler reproof of the ecclesiastical courts? The question had been fought out between Henry II and Becket—a battle of giants: the murder of Becket had caused a revulsion of feeling which left the victory on the ecclesiastical side. But now the problem was being raised again: the first rumblings of a storm which was to burst in fury twenty years later. Whilst More was planning *Utopia*, London had been in a ferment over the question whether clerks in minor orders were to enjoy immunity. The problem, of course, was not limited to England. It had just been declared in the Lateran Council that laymen had no jurisdiction over the clergy,[2] but there were many reasons why discussion was peculiarly acute in London throughout the whole of 1515.

Very characteristically, More sticks to the medieval principle, whilst stripping it of its abuses. Priests in Utopia who commit any offence suffer no temporal punishment; they are left only to God and themselves: "For they think it not lawful to touch him with man's hand, be he never so vicious, who after so singular a sort was dedicate and

---

[2] May 5, 1514.

consecrate to God, as a holy offering." But inconveniences do not result to the State, because in Utopia priests are so few, and so carefully chosen: "of exceeding holiness, and therefore," More grimly says, "very few."

Now, if we read *Utopia* as a modern skit, we may think that this discussion of clerical immunity was introduced merely as an opening for the "satirical observation" that priests of exceeding holiness are very few. That, for example, was how Benjamin Jowett took More's words. They seemed to him to show More's "detestation of priests," and therefore "curiously disagree" with More's life. There is no disagreement. A dozen years later, in his defense of the Church, we find More insisting on selecting priests carefully, and limiting the number. But if, alike in England and in Utopia, the laymen fitted to be made priests are few, that is a reflection, not on the clergy, but on us, the laity: "for of us," says More, "they be made." And he quotes a saying he heard Colet make, many years before, that the clergy will always be one degree better than the laity.

The feeling in London had been embittered by the case of Richard Hunne. Hunne was a prosperous Merchant Taylor of high character, who had a quarrel with the clergy. He was accused of heresy, and whilst in the bishop's prison, awaiting trial, he was found hanged. Had he added the crime of suicide to the crime of heresy? Or had the clergy added the crime of murder to that of false-witness? More was certain that it was a case of suicide. He discussed the matter at length many years after. But popular feeling accused the bishop's officials of murder. Bishop FitzJames of London declared that the Londoners were so set in favor of heresy that a London jury would condemn a clerk "though he were as innocent as Abel." Bishop FitzJames was given to exaggerated language, but, allowing for that, it is clear that there was a good deal of anti-clerical feeling in London at the time. It is all the more noteworthy that so loyal a Londoner as our under-Sheriff should represent the inviolability of the clergy as a sound principle, prescribed by the law of reason which governs Utopia.

We must never forget then that in Utopia the despotic supremacy of the State is balanced by the inviolability of a priesthood entirely exempt from State control.

Another leading problem of controversy was the immortality of the soul. Did philosophy and human reason, apart from revelation, teach such immortality? There were philosophers who said "No"; and, three years before *Utopia* was published, this matter also had come before the Lateran Council.[3] Teachers of philosophy were enjoined to point out how Christian philosophy corrected the views of the heathen on

[3] December 19, 1513: *Concilium Lateranense V, Sessio viii.* See *Conciliorum Omnium tomus XXXIV* (Paris, 1644), pp. 333–35, 557.

immortality; they were to refute these heathen errors, and steps were taken to ensure that the student *in sacris ordinibus constitutus* should not spend more than five years upon philosophy and poetry, before diluting them with the safer studies of theology and pontifical law.

Now, let us try and look at *Utopia* from the point of view of 1516. Here is a heathen community, whose religion is founded on philosophy and natural reason. Yet, so far from doubting the immortality of the soul, they base their whole polity upon it. No disbeliever in immortality may be a citizen of Utopia. In life, and in death, every true Utopian has a firm trust in the communion of saints.

So that, in the eyes of More's friends, Erasmus or Peter Giles, *Utopia* is a striking defense of a vital tenet of the Christian faith. More will not tolerate the ambiguous formula: "As an orthodox Catholic I believe in immortality; as a philosopher I doubt." Reason and philosophy teach the Utopian to affirm that he is somehow in touch with the souls of the noble dead, mighty overseers whose presence encourages him to do his duty the more courageously.

Thus here we find More in *Utopia* opposing the skepticism of his age, precisely as we have seen him opposing its Machiavellian state-craft. And so thoroughly is *Utopia* a book of the hour, that here again More seems to be making a comment on a book which he had never seen. For it was in the very same November of 1516, in which Peter Giles was writing the dedicatory epistle of *Utopia,* that the professor of Philosophy at Bologna, Pomponazzi, published his famous treatise on the Immortality of the Soul. Pomponazzi submitted to the Church in all matters of faith, but, as a philosopher, he stubbornly upheld his doubt concerning the doctrine of immortality.[4]

Therefore More's *Utopia,* among other things, is a contribution to this current controversy. More attacks the enemy in their philosophical camp, and makes his heathen Utopians into unexpected allies of the Catholic faith with regard to this great dogma—and, as we shall see later, with regard to other things as well.

But the imminent problem was monasticism. There was an incompatibility between the declining spirit of the monastic common life, and the rising commercialism of the grasping "new rich." Within a quarter of a century commercialism was to destroy monasticism in England. More stands, as it were, at the crossways, and asks, "Why not destroy commercialism? Is not the spirit of the common life really better worth preserving?" It is significant that *the religious houses are the one European institution which the Utopians are said to approve.* And with reason, for in Utopia, though the rule of celibacy is necessarily absent, the monastic idea is at work. The Utopian

---

[4] The *Tractatus de immortalitate animae* is dated Bologna, November 6, 1516; *Utopia* is dated Antwerp, November 1, 1516.

State is as sumptuous as many a religious house was. But the Utopian, like the monk or friar, may possess nothing. Everyone in Utopia must wear the common habit (in a letter to Erasmus we shall find More calling it Franciscan). There are four varieties, for men and women, married and unmarried. "The cloaks of the Utopians are all of one color, and that is the natural color of the wool." Their hours of work, of recreation, the very games they may play, are all regulated. There are no foolish and pernicious games like dice. Instead, the Utopians have two games, one of which is intended to teach mathematics, and the other to teach morals. The Utopians eat in refectories, beginning every dinner and supper by reading something pertaining to good manners and virtue. Talk at table is initiated and directed by the elders, who graciously encourage the younger married people to join in the discussion, by turning it into a kind of oral examination. As for the men below twenty-two and the girls below eighteen: they serve, or else stand by, in marvellous silence, watching their elders eat and talk.

In much of this, More is perhaps joking; it was his way to utter his jests with such a solemn face as to puzzle his own household. But, underneath More's fun, was a creed as stern as that of Dante, just as, underneath his gold chain, was the shirt of hair. And, quite certainly, the ideal of *Utopia* is discipline, not liberty. It is influenced by some of the most severe disciplines the world has ever known. Through Plato's *Republic* it goes back to the barracks life of a Spartan warrior through More's own experience to the life of a Charterhouse monk. And the discipline of Utopia is enforced rigidly, even ferociously. If the Utopian attempts to break the laws of his native land, there is the penalty of bondage, and, if that fails, of death. We have seen that even to speak of State affairs, except at the licensed place and hour, is punishable in Utopia with death, lest permission to discuss politics might lead to revolution. Has any State, at any time, carried terrorism quite so far?

Many framers of ideal commonwealths have shirked the question of compulsion, by imagining their citizens to have all become moral overnight. More does not choose this easy way. He recognizes that there will be a minority, to whom higher motives do not appeal. For them, there is penal servitude; if that fails, death.

But no great State can be founded on terrorism. For the mass of its citizens, Utopia is founded on religious enthusiasm. Faith in God, and in the immortal destiny of the human soul, supplies the driving power which is to quench human passion and human greed. Based on religion, Utopia is supported by a belief in the dignity of manual labor. Even rulers and magistrates, although legally exempt, share in this work as an example to others. So a six-hours' day suffices, and the rest of the time is free for those intellectual and artistic pursuits in which, to the Utopians, pleasure consists. But religion is the basis of all.

Now a monk of today, Dom Ursmer Berlière, of the Abbey of Maredsous, has pointed out how at the beginning of the Middle Ages, monasticism, as St. Benedict shaped it, gave a pattern to the State. St. Benedict's monastery "was a little State, which could serve as a model for the new Christian society which was arising from the fusion of the conquered and conquering races—a little State which had for its basis, religion; for its support, the honor given to work; for its crown, a new intellectual and artistic culture." [5] The writer was not thinking of *Utopia*. I do not know if he had ever read it. But, at the end of the Middle Ages, we find More depicting a State founded on just these things: the common life, based on religion; honor given to manual labor; intellectual and artistic culture. However far these things might sometimes be from monastic practice, the writer of *Utopia* could never have approved of the destruction of monasticism; he looked for its reform.

And, just as the customs of Utopia have their bearing on the urgent questions of the time, so has the framework of the book—the story of the travels and circumnavigation of Raphael Hythloday. We have only to look at a globe—a flat Mercator's map conceals the fact—to see how the destiny of England had been shaped by the discovery of the New World. England, till More's day remote from the center of things, and unable to employ very profitably the skill of her mariners, was now found to be peculiarly well placed. The farther from the Equator, the shorter the way round the world. A similar favorable situation had enabled the Norsemen to discover America five centuries before, though they could not exploit their discovery. But now Englishmen were bound to seek for a northwest passage to Japan, China, and India. True, America blocked their way. But this only meant that they found something even better than they sought. And so, under an Italian captain, resident in Bristol, Bristol men in a Bristol ship first discovered the mainland of America, with authority to set up the royal banners of Henry VII in "any village, town, castle, island or mainland of them newly found," and to import into England free of customs any merchandise they might get there. If every man had his due, America would be called Cabota; and Henry VII, rather than a modern peer, would be hailed as the first Crusader for Empire Free Trade. But Cabot had a bad press, or rather no press at all; the new art of printing spread the fame of a later explorer, Amerigo Vespucci; so Amerigo became godfather of the new continent, and, as we have

[5] Dom Ursmer Berlière, *L'orde monastique des origines au XIIe. siècle,* 2nd ed. (Paris: Lethielleux, 1921), p. 45.

seen, it was *his* travels, "now in print and abroad in every man's hands," which inspired Thomas More.

Yet recent research has shown that More had also domestic inspiration.

More was about nineteen when John Cabot discovered the mainland of America. During the rest of the reign of Henry VII transatlantic exploration was kept before men's eyes. The "Company Adventurers into the New Found Lands" were busy at Bristol. About 1502, three specimen savages, clothed in skins and eating raw flesh, were presented to the King. Two years later, two of them were still to be seen about the Palace at Westminster, clothed and looking like Englishmen. More had probably seen them, and wondered what thoughts lay behind their inscrutable faces. In 1505 "wild cats and popinjays of the New-found Island" were brought to the King at Richmond. In the last year of the reign of Henry VII, Sebastian Cabot went in search of the Northwest Passage. It seems clear that he penetrated the strait later known by the name of Hudson, and found it opening into the immense expanse which we call Hudson Bay. Such an anticipation by Cabot, in 1509, of later Elizabethan and even Stuart exploration seems almost incredible. Yet "if he was lying, he had the devil's own luck. For we know now that the facts are substantially as he represented them." [6] Cabot naturally assumed that Hudson Bay was what we call the Pacific, and consequently that he had discovered the Northwest Passage. He returned to England with the glorious secret to find Henry VII dead, and Henry VIII and Wolsey obsessed with their continental schemes. After three years of disappointment, Sebastian left England and entered the Spanish service. He lived nearly fifty years longer without ever having an opportunity of finding that his magnificent discovery was only a dead end. For him, perhaps it was as well that he was not destined to be numbered among the "frozen pilots" upon whose funeral the Arctic stars have looked down. But the cessation of North American exploration meant that for England valuable experience was lost, the work of Henry VII was undone, and England was "beaten back from the seas into the dusty vortex of European politics." [7]

Yet there were still Englishmen who understood the importance of transatlantic adventure, and Professor A. W. Reed's research into the circle of Thomas More has brought to light the story of the first attempt at the colonization of North America by England. Six months after the publication of *Utopia,* More's brother-in-law, John Rastell, set off on the *Barbara* of Greenwich on a voyage of discovery to the

[6] J. A. Williamson, *The Voyages of the Cabots* (London: The Argonaut Press, 1929), p. 241.

[7] Geoffrey A. R. Callender, *The Naval Side of British History* (London: Christophers, 1924), p. 47.

New Found Lands. That not merely exploration, but the establishment of some kind of settlement was in his mind, follows from the
fact that he took "tools for masons and carpenters, and other engines
that he had prepared for the New Lands." John Rastell expected to be
away for three years, during which he had arranged by prepayment
that Judge John More should keep his wife and servants. Judge More
seems to have taken a large share in guaranteeing the venture. The
expedition turned back, owing to an organized mutiny, which appar-
ently had the approval of the Earl of Surrey, the Lord High Admiral,
who was opposed to sending any part of the fleet across the Atlantic
when it might be needed in the Channel. Spirited interference in continental politics did not allow of valuable fighting ships being sent on
voyages of exploration, likely to last three years.

Now every reader of *Utopia* must be struck by the weight there
placed on colonization. The Utopians hate war: "War they do detest
and abhor; and contrary to the custom almost of all other nations,
they count nothing so much against glory, as glory gotten in war." But
to secure colonies for an overflowing population, they consider that
even war is justified "by the law of nature." "For they count this the
most just cause of war, when any people holdeth a piece of ground
void and vacant, to no good nor profitable use, keeping others from
the use and possession of it."

All this sounds so imperialistic that some foreign critics have seen
in Thomas More one further typical perfidious Englishman, who (with
a Machiavellism more subtle than that of Machiavelli himself) pro-
pounded exactly such pretexts for expansion as would be useful to the
British Empire of future centuries, and who yet, with characteristic
English hypocrisy, pretended to be fighting for morality all the time.

But, when More emphasizes that the Utopians only go to war for
reasons which concern the welfare of their citizens or of their allies, he
is wishing to get in a side blow at the state of Europe in 1516, and to
censure wars waged at the whim of, and for the personal aggrandizement of, autocrats like Francis I, or Henry, or Wolsey. I admit that the
reasons for warfare approved by the Utopians, if made into a code, and
applied to history from the seventeenth century to the present day,
would load the dice heavily in favor of the British Empire; for they are
adapted to a great colonizing island State, such as Utopia is supposed
to be, and such as Britain later became. But could More, with all his
foresight, have foreseen all this?

One recent German historian[8] has suggested that More, when he
makes the Utopians claim the right as a populous nation to colonize

[8] Hermann Oncken, "Die Utopia des Thomas Morus und das Machtproblem in
der Staatslehre," *Sitzungsberichte der Heidelberger Akademie, Phil.-Hist. Klasse,*
1922.

empty spaces, may have been thinking of English settlements in North America. Another[9] argues that these theories of the natural right of colonization are no part of the original description of Utopia, already written in 1515; they do not harmonize with it, he thinks, but are a later addition made in 1516. And it must be admitted that this is acute criticism, for these German historians were quite unaware of Professor Reed's discovery; it had not been published when they wrote. And it is certain that John Rastell was not thinking merely of the Northwest Passage to the Indies. He describes his object at some length. He wants *colonization:* that Englishmen should make "first building and habitation" in the lands Cabot had discovered; that the king should have his "dominion extending into so far a ground," that the heathen should be evangelized. The trade Rastell thinks of is not in oriental spices, gold or jewels, but in the products of the North American coast —timber, pitch, tar, and above all fish. But, he complains, the French are getting there before us: "yearly of fish there they [the French] lade above an hundred sail." [10]

The moment was favorable. Of course Englishmen could only at their peril trespass in the Spanish Indies; but there was nothing to hinder them from exploiting the claim which the wise Henry VII had staked out in the North. The Spaniards had enough to do in the warm water, without venturing among the ice-floes. Charles V could not, and would not, quarrel with England over a claim which was of no use to him. Indeed he would not quarrel with England over much more important matters; for he had his life-long feud with Francis of France, and if Henry had sided with Francis they could together have closed the English Channel against him, and cut off his dominions in the Netherlands from his dominions in Spain. So the way for exploration in North America lay open to England. But Henry and Wolsey, absorbed in winning "ungracious dogholes" in France, had none of the curiosity about Atlantic adventure which More and Rastell felt. Later, in 1521, Henry showed a transient interest in the New Found Land. It has been suggested that this was due to More, then rising in the king's favor, and discussing with him Geometry and Astronomy (and probably Cosmography). But the French war of 1522 stopped this, as it stopped other useful schemes. Expeditions did indeed set out in 1527 and 1536. The explorers found Portuguese, Breton and Norman vessels before them in the New World, but did nothing useful themselves. North American exploration was left to Jacques Cartier and the French.

[9] Ernst Tröltsch, *Christian Thought: Its History and Application* (London: University of London Press, 1923), pp. 145ff.

[10] John Rastell, *The Interlude of the Four Elements* (London: for the Percy Society, 1848), pp. 30–31.

Although we need not follow More's German critics in making him the father of British Imperialism, the discovery of Rastell's venture does prove that this criticism has a certain element of truth. Colonization and transatlantic adventure meant much to the writer of *Utopia*.

Yet there is nothing so sinister about it as as these German critics have argued. The Utopians only settle where there is "much waste and unoccupied ground," and they admit to full citizenship any of the natives who care to join them. It would have been well if all sixteenth-century colonization had been equally humane. And More's words cannot be twisted into a plea for a monopoly of colonial rights for England; if he is staking out a claim, it is for the common body of Christendom. For *Utopia* is a work of our common Western European civilization, dedicated to subjects of Charles V, Giles and Busleiden, the Latin text published in six great European cities before it was ever published in England, and translated into German, Italian, and French before, in 1551, the English translation appeared.

We can only understand *Utopia* if we remember the Europe for which it was written; at home John Rastell preaching exploration to the More household; abroad the travels of Vespucci in every man's hands; Vespucci, who had found folk holding property in common, and not esteeming gold, pearls, or jewels. (It is important to remember that the Inca empire of Peru, which in more than one detail had a likeness to Utopia, was not known till some fourteen years later; Cortes had not yet conquered Mexico.)

The problem of poverty and unemployment (destined in England to be aggravated by the Dissolution of the Monasteries) was already a European one. Ten years after *Utopia*, More's friend Vives wrote a tract on it. At the root of More's interest in colonization lies his pity for the unemployed laborers:

> Poor silly wretched souls; away they trudge out of their known and accustomed houses; all their household stuff, being suddenly thrust out, they be constrained to sell it for a thing of naught. And when they have, wandering about, soon spent that, what can they do but steal, and then be hanged, or else go about abegging. Whom no man will set awork, though they never so willingly offer themselves thereto.

But the fact that *Utopia* belongs to its age does not mean that it is the less epoch-making. Some things which may now seem commonplaces to us were less so then. It may seem quite natural to us that in Utopia there should be no class distinctions. It was less obvious to a scholar of the Renaissance. Plato's Commonwealths had been based on class distinction. In the *Laws* the citizens fall into four classes. In the *Republic*, also, there are classes, although so much attention is given to the warrior class, and their common life, that we almost forget the others. Plato is emphatic that every man should have one job only, and he does not waste words on his artisans, except to urge that they must be experts in their own business, and must stick to it. The Middle Ages inherited the same idea of the State: ploughmen and artisans to labor, clerks to pray and study, knights to fight. But the Utopian citizen does all three things; he labors with his hands, studies in his spare hours, and, though he hates warfare, is, at need, a soldier.

It is noteworthy that, despite his admiration for Greek life and thought, More did not build Utopia after the Hellenic pattern. His free citizens are not a privileged class dependent on slave labor, nor are his bondmen a distinct class. Bondage in Utopia is penal servitude —a humane substitute for the death penalty. The repentant bondman is restored to freedom, the incorrigible bondman is slain. But the citizens themselves are all workers.

Finally the outstanding feature of *Utopia* is implied in the great sentence with which Raphael ends his story:

> When I consider all these commonwealths which nowadays anywhere do flourish, so God help me, I can perceive nothing but a conspiracy of rich men, procuring their own commodities under the name and title of the commonwealth.

The Middle Ages had often been charitable to the poor, and More's age had inherited vast charitable endowments. More altogether approved of these endowments, and, later, we shall find him defending them against the fanaticism of reformers who wished to hand them over to a conspiracy of rich men procuring their own commodities under the title of the commonwealth. But More's claim for *justice* goes far beyond medieval admonitions to charity. Its publication throughout Europe by the printing press marks an epoch.

# A Moral Fable

## by H. W. Donner

The Utopian commonwealth is ingeniously built up from suggestions in the narratives of Vespucci and Peter Martyr, combined with
hints from Plato's *Republic* and *Laws,* the *Germania* of Tacitus, and
other sources which describe the workings of a primitive society, if by
primitive is meant a society living according to the law of nature. All
Utopian institutions are founded on reason, and on reason alone. More
has been careful never to exceed this self-imposed limitation. The
Utopians have learned everything that the ancient philosophers can
teach us, and even in their religion there is nothing for which there
was no precedent in classical antiquity. Like their institutions, their
philosophy and religion also are founded on reason. Their virtue consists in living according to nature, and the law of nature regulates their
private and public life, their actions in peace as well as in war. As a
synthesis of the best pagan customs and philosophical systems, of the
political and religious thought of the pagan world, Utopia is an
achievement of no small significance, a *tour de force* which delighted
the humanists of the Renaissance and gained for its author a position
among the foremost men of learning in Europe, excelling in wit,
erudition, and style. To the learned it was not least for its scholarship
that *Utopia* became an object of admiration. With a consistency that
must impress minds trained in the school of the Platonic Academy of
Florence and stimulated by the constructions of Pico and Reuchlin,
More assigned to the Utopians a definite place in the order of the
universe and in the history of mankind. To the common reader no
such complexities need detract from his enjoyment of the book as a
production of humanist wit, a *jeu d'esprit* of an uncommonly accessi-
ble nature.

Against the background of Europe ruled by Folly, as described by
Erasmus in the *Moriae Encomium* or by More himself in the first book,
Utopia is described as ruled by Reason. It is a picture that must stimu-

*From H. W. Donner,* Introduction to Utopia *(London: Sidgwick and Jackson, Ltd.,
1945), pp. 75–83. Copyright © Sidgwick and Jackson, Ltd., 1946. Reprinted by permission of the publisher.*

late even the most unthinking to some searching of heart. As the late
R. W. Chambers put it, "the virtues of heathen Utopia show up by
contrast the vices of Christian Europe." It is as a plea for Reason that
the *Utopia* must strike the reader most forcibly. Against the background of insane tyranny and senseless war, Utopia enjoys both peace
and freedom. Instead of lawlessness and anarchy in Europe, law and
order in Utopia. It is an order based on respect for the dignity of man
and the freedom of conscience, trampled under foot in contemporary
Europe. Instead of the selfishness and greed of a few rich men depriv-
ing the European masses of their means of livelihood, collaboration
for the common good providing plenty for all Utopian citizens. Instead
of concentrating on material gains, the Utopians prefer the pleasures of
the mind. Learning is there the property of all, whereas in Europe
ignorance in the cloak of priesthood was persistently trying to stop the
expansion of the mind. In Utopia there is no such contradiction, and,
in words strongly reminiscent of Pico, More sets out the Utopian conviction of the agreement between the conclusions of an enquiring reason and the truths of a divinely inspired religion.

> For whilst they by the help of this Philosophy search out the secret
> mysteries of nature, they think that they not only receive thereby won-
> derful great pleasure, but also obtain great thanks and favour of the
> author and maker thereof. Whom they think, according to the fashion
> of other artificers, to have set forth the marvellous and gorgeous frame of
> the world for man to behold; whom only he hath made of wit and ca-
> pacity to consider and understand the excellency of so great a work. And
> therefore, say they, doth he bear more good will and love to the curious
> and diligent beholder and viewer of his work, and marvellor at the same,
> than he doth to him, which like a very beast without wit and reason, or
> as one without sense or moving, hath no regard to so great and so won-
> derful a spectacle.

Lest, however, we should be misled by the parallel to disapprove of the
religious orders as such, More has given Utopia her monks also, who
prefer hard manual labor to the contemplation of nature. For even the
Utopians recognize that reason is not sufficient for the understanding
of all mysteries in nature, and so in their philosophy they call on
religion for the confirmation of the fundamental truth of the existence
of God and man's immortality, postulated by reason. While from the
nature of his sources he had to make his Utopians embrace an Epicurean doctrine of pleasure which might seem to conflict with the
medieval ideal of asceticism, More with his supreme intellectual facility
dissolves the difficulty by making them recognize the insufficiency of
reason to decide in what the felicity of man consists and so they come
naturally to found morality on religion.

They reason of virtue and pleasure. But the chief and principal question is in what thing, be it one or more, the felicity of man consisteth. But in this point they seem almost too much given and inclined to the opinion of them which defend pleasure; wherein they determine either all or the chiefest part of man's felicity to rest. And (which is more to be marvelled at) the defence of this so dainty and delicate an opinion they fetch even from their grave, sharp, bitter, and rigorous religion. For they never dispute of felicity or blessedness, but they join to the reasons of Philosophy certain principles taken out of religion; without the which, to the investigation of true felicity, they think reason of itself weak and unperfect.

It is in the spirit that inspires the Utopian commonwealth that we must seek the key to the interpretation of its meaning. This is to be found neither in its laws nor in its institutions. Utopia is not a country where everybody acts reasonably from choice only, but under a compulsion intolerable to modern minds. Utopian law is indeed a law as "ungentle and sharp" as it is inexorable. To Europe, however, God has given "the new law of clemency and mercy, under the which he ruleth us with fatherly gentleness, as his dear children." In our appreciation of Utopia we must consequently understand that her citizens labor under the handicap of that "ungentle and sharp law" which reflects their "grave, sharp, bitter, and rigorous religion," whereas to us Christians God has given not only reason to guide us, but he has also revealed to us his own law, which is love, and peace, and justice.

"Reason is servant to Faith and not enemy," said More, and so faith rises on the foundations of reason, like the pinnacles and spires from the roof of a cathedral. But reason alone can never arrive at the "fruition of the sight of God's glorious majesty face to face." To a disciple of St. Thomas Aquinas, Pico, and Colet, the most elevated pagan philosophy and religion could only be a preparation for the revelation of Christianity, and the first rungs on Jacob's ladder. The law of reason, which governs Utopia, is subservient to the Divine law, which ought to rule the behavior of all Christians. Raphael Hythloday consequently tells us that we must not "wink at the most part of all those things which Christ taught us and so straitly forbade them to be winked at, that those things also which he whispered in the ears of his disciples, he commanded to be proclaimed openly on the house-tops." However ideal it might appear by contrast with the contemporary Europe, Utopia does not represent More's ultimate ideal. It is a state founded only upon reason and ruled by the "ungentle and sharp" law of nature. It does not embody the religion of Christ with its "new law of clemency and mercy." It is a state where slavery is permitted, although in a milder form than in classical antiquity, but it is not a state where all are brethren, as Christ would have it. It is a community where grievous offences against the law are punished with death, but "God commandeth us that we shall not kill."

Reason by itself is "weak and unperfect." Only God's guidance can bring man to the perfection for which He created him. Hence pagan behavior cannot be a model for Christians to imitate, or as Erasmus put it in his *Institutio principis Christiani*: "Whenever you think of yourself as a prince, remember that you are a Christian prince! You should be as different from even the noble pagan princes as a Christian is from a pagan." Providence had not granted to the Utopians the privilege of Revelation, and so their manners cannot serve as models for those who have received revealed religion, even if the Utopian welcome extended to the Christians in Hythloday's party seems to indicate that they have not much farther to travel on the road of preparation for the reception of the mystery. So far they remain on the level of pagan philosophy, and the ultimate ideal is very much higher. Speaking of the great princes of antiquity, Erasmus says: "As it would be most disgraceful to be surpassed by them in any honorable deed of theirs, so it would be the last degree of madness for a Christian prince to wish to imitate them without change." The disgrace of being surpassed by the heathen was keenly felt by Vives in comparing the *Legenda Aurea* with the classical masterpieces of literature, relating not the lives of saints but of cruel soldiers and generals. Yet how much greater shame must not we feel, seeing that whereas we live at constant enmity one against the other, the Utopians have achieved a state of law and order. In spite of their hard laws they have surpassed us, not only in the perfection of their institutions, but in their mutual help and generosity and unreserved collaboration. Even in the instance of punishments they seem to have surpassed us, for whereas the Utopians inflict capital punishment only on hardened sinners, Europeans punish the loss of a little money with "the loss of man's life." In this manner of interpretation Raphael's arguments in the first book of *Utopia* derive the strongest possible support from the institutions of the Utopians, not in the likeness but in the differences between a Christian and a pagan state. Whereas the pagan Utopians may employ serfs to meet the needs of labor, the disgrace to Europe is almost inconceivable inasmuch as servitude in Utopia should be found preferable to so called "freedom" elsewhere. In attempting to understand More's meaning we must always remember this, that reason alone supports the Utopian laws and institutions, but reason has a claim on Europe also. It is not enemy to Faith, but servant. In the likeness of Utopia More shows how certain institutions in Europe, threatened by destruction, are founded on reason and so worth preserving, because where there is reason there is hope of religion. But for Christians to try and imitate

Utopian institutions without change "would be the last degree of madness."

When therefore sociologists are concerned to show to what extent the Utopian ideal has been realized in modern society and to what degree it still remains unfulfilled, they are merely breaking up the Colosseum in order to build the Farnese Palace. They have seen only the stones and forgotten the vision. It was not the constitution of commonwealths that More desired to reform, but the spirit. The Utopian institutions can be nothing except "very absurd" without the spirit that informs them. They must not be copied, but surpassed by Christian institutions. The community of goods that reason recommends to the Utopians, must be excelled in the spiritual community of all Christians. It was the Christian monasteries that provided the pattern for the Utopian republic, and in More's mind it was they that represented the mundane revelation of the ultimate ideal.

It might be exemplified in concrete instances how far short of the Christian standard the Utopians actually fall. When the priests in Utopia are allowed to marry, this must not be understood as More's scheme for the reformation of the Church; it is merely that God has not granted them that personal intimacy which has only been made possible through the Incarnation. Utopian religious customs are no more models for the Christian Church than are the political institutions of that commonwealth, and so must not be taken literally. The fact that in Utopia God is worshipped under different names, is certainly not served up by More for imitation by the Catholic Church, to which in More's view God had alone revealed himself. The Utopians with reason as their sole guide can only convince themselves of the existence of God; about his nature they can know nothing. Hence toleration is natural to them. Yet I cannot agree with those who would have it not apply where Christianity is concerned, being a revealed religion and so admitting of no doubt as to the truth of its doctrine. The Divine law is a law "of clemency and mercy," and the Utopian toleration requires its counterpart in Christian charity. Whatever ideas he may have entertained concerning the reformation of the Church, and it would carry us too far to go into the question of its details, More left it to the Church itself. Even in the first part of *Utopia* where he so sharply criticizes European conditions, not sparing ecclesiastics any more than laymen, it is the abuses he condemns, not the institutions. What he is asking for, is that in the same way as reason was allowed to regulate life in Utopia, so reason illuminated by Divine revelation should be given a hearing in European affairs. Just as the Utopians live in strict obedience to the law of nature, so must we be ruled by the law of Christ. Temporal justice is "the strongest and surest bond of commonwealth," says More, and he does not want us to set it aside, but man-made law must be tempered by the law of Christ which is itself the highest justice.

Such has long been the Roman Catholic interpretation of *Utopia*, and it has been convincingly restated during recent years. It has been maintained with characteristic vigor and eloquence by the late R. W. Chambers in his great biography of More. This was also the way in which his contemporaries understood More's intention, as plainly appears from Budé's remark that if only the three principles of Utopia, which he accurately defined as equality, love of peace, and contempt of gold, could be "fixed in the minds of all men, . . . We should soon see pride, covetousness, insane competition, and almost all other deadly weapons of our adversary the devil, fall powerless." By showing how far short of the Utopians contemporary Europe fell in the practice of the four cardinal virtues of wisdom, fortitude, temperance, and justice, More wanted to stimulate us not only in the exercise of mundane virtue but of the Christian virtues also of faith, hope, and charity. In St. Augustine's terminology we may say that in Utopia More gives us such a description of a *vita socialis*, based only on the four pagan virtues, as must most forcibly remind us of our duty by means of an ardent exercise of the three Christian virtues to prepare for the *Civitas Dei*. Self-love, according to St. Augustine, is the opposite to the love of God, and so it is the love of self in all its utterances from mere vanity to cruel tyranny that More attacks most violently in the first book of Utopia, showing us in the second how the noble Utopians have eschewed self from all their dealings and find their greatest pleasure in working for the good of all and in actively helping their fellows. We cling to our worldly treasure, but the Utopians gladly give up their houses every ten years. More does not want us to imitate this custom, which no doubt he would have described as "very absurd," but he did want us to feel that one house is "as nigh heaven" as another. More did not want us to give everything away, but he did want us to use our wealth in such a way that it should not be said that in our states "money beareth all the stroke"; not for the increase of our own luxury, but for the relief of poverty, so that the prosperity of our society might rival that of Utopia itself. The love of power, which in the guise of the new Machiavellian statecraft was ruining Europe, was in More's view but another outcome of the love of self. In Utopia, however, aggressors are so cruelly punished that they are not likely to disturb the peace a second time.

Religion must reinforce the arguments of reason and Christian society surpass the pagan. It is not our institutions that we must destroy, but those evil passions which are at the root of the abuses. More's program of reform was one of personal amelioration. "There is nothing better," John Colet, his teacher and confessor, had written to Erasmus, "than that we should lead a pure and holy life, which in my judgment will never be attained but by the ardent love and imitation of Jesus." Had not St. Matthew told us also, that "the disciple is not above his master, nor the servant above his lord." More had not forgotten the lesson, and his own passion bears witness to his pious striving to imitate his Master.

In his *Apology* More did not omit pointing to the personal responsibility of each individual for the good of all. Speaking of the "faults, enormities, and errors" that beset both state and church, he says these he would wish to have amended, "and every man specially labor to mend himself." This is the advice also that Raphael Hythloday would have wished to give his king—to "let him rather amend his own life, renounce unhonest pleasures, and forsake pride." And in the next instance More asks all to work together to eliminate the faults of society, "observed in the doing evermore such order and fashion as may stand and agree with reason and justice, the king's laws of the realm, the Scripture of God, and the laws of Christ's Church, ever keeping love and concord. . . . This has been hitherto the whole sum of my writing." Neither did More neglect to rub in the lesson, "for I think every man's duty toward God is so great, that very few folk serve him as they should do."

If, then, one should want to sum up the *Utopia* in a few inadequate words—for the subject is interminable—one may say that:

In the first book More analyzes the evils that beset early sixteenth century English society—and to some extent these are the evils of all human society—and makes suggestions how they might be mitigated. The second book is a moral fable, intended to delight with its wit and ingenuity while it teaches a lesson in private and public morals by means of an example. It does not describe the ultimate ideal, but one that is practicable enough, which we are asked not slavishly to copy, but to surpass and excel. The *Utopia* does not attempt a final solution of the problems of human society—for More was too wise to attempt the impossible—but it contains an appeal addressed to all of us, which allows of no refusal, that we should try and do each one his share to mend our own selves and ease the burden of our fellow-men, to improve mankind and prepare for the life to come. In this lies its enduring power, that however high we may fix the ideal, to whatever perfection we may attain, More points higher still, from matter to the spirit, and from man to God.

# *Utopia* and Power Politics

## *by Gerhard Ritter*

Thomas More dared to describe in all its details the life led by a community in the Golden Age. Utopia, this lonely island somewhere in the vast expanse of the ocean, had preserved these features undistorted by European influence to this day.[1] The language of the Utopians indicated that they derived directly from the Greeks. And the keenness with which they adopted Christianity—Raphael Hythloday brought it to their island—confirmed in the most beautiful manner that it was but a higher form of the ancient philosophy and did not contradict Greek thought in any way. The medieval teaching of gradual progress was applied to the relationship of pre-Christian, "natural" human wisdom and Christian revelation.[2] He did not even notice the —politically—most important difference between the ancient religions and Christianity, namely the fact that the Greek gods were gods of the city, of the State, and that there was no special caste of priests. More, quite innocently, granted the Utopian priests the same independence from the State as was claimed by the Roman Catholic hierarchy. The indissoluble connection of the Greeks with the law and faith of the community was transformed in his hands into the freedom of thought of his Utopians, an attitude which led to a fairly far-reaching tolerance exercised by the State. He did not know that he had thus destroyed the harmonious unity of the Greek city state.

Satisfied that classical and Christian heritage were in harmony More wrote the second book of his *Utopia* to describe this happy island. The work of glorious imagination, it shows signs of genius even if his invention did not allow a well-ordered scheme nor prevented repetitions and overlapping. The whole was a wonderful satire that poked fun at contemporary institutions and events, was full of allusions, hidden bite and, presumably, intentionally grotesque features which made fun

---

*From Gerhard Ritter,* The Corrupting Influence of Power *(6th ed.), trans. F. W. Pick (Hadleigh, Essex, England: Tower Bridge Publications, 1952), pp. 70–89.*

[1] Perhaps Vespucci's accounts of American tribes with communal property had given More the idea of making use of his motive.

[2] What strikes the reader today as modern secularism must be considered pre-Christian rather: it is to lead up to the transcendental Christian revelation.

of the reader and pulled his leg. Erasmus has told us that his friend spent considerable time over it. Only after completion of the whole work did he probably realize what an abyss opened up between this ideal island and his own surroundings, a contrast which had formed the starting point of the whole conception. This realization must have been overpowering and saddening. What had been begun as a gay satire ended in a bitter, even desperate indictment of English society and the State. This part was written, and again it was Erasmus who has told us so, in all haste, most likely as the result of his discussions with his friends during his Mission to the Low Countries. It was only then that he touched the question which appeared suddenly to become of vital importance—whether there was any hope that the ideals of the Utopian welfare State could ever become a reality in Europe. His doubts, and the dualism that gripped him, appeared in all their oppressiveness in this desperate question and his attempt to answer it.

Yet, More did not resign himself to the world as he found it. If he could not hope for the realization of his dreams, he continued to desire that some at least of his Utopian institutions would be imitated in Europe. His satire was no simple dance of satyrs. It represented some of his dearest dreams. He expressed, e.g., the wish for the reign of the literary educated, the philosophers in the State. They were not thought of as a separate class but continually renewed themselves through gaining fresh recruits from other groups; they were an elite of the intellectually gifted and the morally most advanced. They resembled Plato's philosophers, an aristocracy who had overcome mean ambitions and passions. Out of their midst the highest officials of the State—ambassadors, priests, senators, even the princes themselves—should be chosen by election. Next, there was More's insistence on safeguarding the liberties of the people against the arbitrariness and tyranny of the rulers: he provided for frequent changes of office holders, banned all secret deliberations about political questions, all formation of cliques which could endanger civil liberties, and insisted that the people ought to be asked their opinions frequently by the lower officials.

He looked forward to an improvement of the position of the common man through an absolutely fair and just distribution of consumer's goods, severe limitation of working hours, grand public welfare institutions and educational facilities, a mild penal code, the abolition of all class distinction before the law. It was true, he admitted unfree slaves who were recruited from criminals and prisoners of war; but nobody was born a slave and no separate class could thus emerge. Nor, of course, could anybody be born into the group of the literary, educated elite. All in all, this was a rational constitution. Its frills, of course, were so dainty and often laughable, and could not

form the model for a European constitutional State. But the purpose of
the whole structure was obvious and was meant, in all seriousness, to
do just this: to provide the framework for a nation which suppresses
selfishness with all possible means by developing educational and all
kinds of social institutions, it was meant to show the working of a
State which renounced foreign conquests, as far as at all possible, and
served exclusively the intellectual and general welfare of the community.

Was it possible for any State to renounce all expansive aims abroad?
Could there be a State without continual struggle for power? Could it
be secure from foreign intervention without being powerful? How
serious More was when he wrote his *Utopia* is proved by the fact that
he did not avoid these questions as Erasmus had done. He tried to
answer them. And his discussion of the nature of power revealed the
unresolved problems of his political theory. At the same time, he shed
new light on the demonic character of power and the State of today.

Utopia was an island. Its politics therefore were insular in character.
Splendid ports made communication with foreign countries easy; but
these harbors were well defended, either naturally or by strong fortifi-
cations so that it would be difficult for foreign troops to land there.
Utopia was not exposed to the rival claims of other Powers as were
European States in their closely packed continent. It did not find itself
surrounded by continually threatening neighbors. It did not need to
spend the main part of its energies as a State on military preparations;
nor was it continually tempted to take a hand in conquest, at least not
in the continental style. Utopia's frontiers were clearly drawn by nature
—along the water's edge. Beyond that it could exercise influence only
in an indirect manner, by the acquisition for instance of colonies or
by its economic power. These were the conditions necessary for More
to make the welfare of the population the center of all Utopian politics. The feudal monarchies of Europe, on the other hand, had to
survive without any of these pre-conditions being fulfilled. The Utopians found it easier than other nations to remain untainted by selfishness and brutal power politics. Naturally, Thomas More, the Englishman, thought all along of his own country.

However, neither Great Britain nor Utopia were completely separated from the outside world. Utopia remained threatened, if to a
lesser degree than continental States, by foreign invasion. That was
why its towns and its beaches were well fortified (a warning for England?); that was why its people were asked continuously, especially on
holidays, to undertake military training and to maintain a huge war-
chest so as to be ready for any emergency. More could not visualize the
complete isolation of his island because, amongst other things, he was
intent on showing what methods ought to be employed by a sane

foreign policy; he wanted to establish a model which he could sharply contrast to the unreasonableness of the feudal rulers in Europe.

What was this model foreign policy like? Fundamentally, More was out to avoid all the mistakes which he found repulsive in the political methods of the European courts. This meant: no conquests and no selfish suppression of the independence of other nations; arbitration and peaceful negotiations, as far as at all possible, were to replace the use of brute force. Why indeed should Utopians want to conquer any foreign people and suppress their liberties and independence? This happy island was well content with its own "living space." Economically it was almost self-contained. But for iron ore which had to be imported, since there was not enough of it on the island itself (and in this it also resembled the British Isles), everything else wanted by Utopians could be gained in abundance from their own soil. There was a gigantic surplus in wheat, honey, wool, linen, timber, dyes, wax, tallow, leather and cattle; of this they exported whenever their own requirements for the next two years were secure. This export trade was their chief connection with countries overseas. It led to a strongly active trade balance, hence to increasing silver and gold hoards which they accepted in payment.

This amassing of overwhelming economic power was assuredly putting temptation into their way. Would such wealth lead to a moral decline? The Utopians realized the danger they ran and manfully set about to meet it. In order to make gold and silver despicable they declared it, with the help of official propaganda, to be useless and worthless; it was thought ridiculous to use gold or precious stones as jewelry; chamber pots were made of gold, and so were the chains for slaves; pearls and diamonds were given to the children to play with— foreigners, who saw this, could not help being taken by surprise and to find themselves often in awkward and amusing positions. More used all his satirical gifts to describe these scenes. But was he serious in this or joking? How could the Utopians think so little of gold if they accepted it in payment from abroad! In truth, his jollity covered up the fact that he did not know the answer to this problem. He could not deny that the wealth of the whole people exerted an influence on the living standard of every citizen; nor, that effortless gain must undermine the simplicity of their life and ethics—a simplicity which he cherished for his Utopians despite the refinement of their aristocracy.

However, he knew of yet another method of countering a decline in the moral standard of the community: he did away with private property. All profits from overseas trade belonged to the State; and it was the duty of the State to see to it that as little precious metal as possible entered Utopia, and that most of what had to be admitted was kept in the chancellor's chest. A seventh of the profits was anyway

given to the poor of the seller's country; prices were kept low and
profits were partly reinvested in imports; only a small part was reserved for the State chest (in cash, i.e., in gold or silver); the rest was
left abroad in the form of credits, especially as loans placed at the
disposal of towns and cities abroad—and they need not worry about
the interest rate! Interest, indeed, was asked for in exceptional cases
only, namely when the Utopians required money to grant loans to
other countries or, in case of war, to pay hired soldiers or to buy their
enemies or cause them to fight one another, i.e., to sow discord and
pay for treachery.

This showed the helplessness, and hopelessness, of More's attempt
to find the basis of a foreign policy which needed neither power nor
the means of the struggle for power. In order to avoid rivalry and
real struggle More gave his Utopians a flying start by granting them
undoubted economic superiority over all their neighbors. But he
appeared blissfully unaware—and one cannot doubt his sincerity—of
the fact that he had placed them into such a position of overwhelming strength, had endowed them with a political power which must
have been a threat in the eyes of their neighbors; it was really asking
for trouble and abuse of power. If every other country was indebted
to Utopia, how else could its neighbors view the position than as
one that endangered their own position? And debts kept on increasing;
there was no guarantee that the rulers of Amaurote, the island capital,
would not abuse their power, increase the prices charged or stop giving
away export goods (which, anyway, appeared to be too good an action
to be true). Moreover, which self-respecting nation would like to
receive such presents forever? Obviously the neighbors were forced
to buy Utopian goods; otherwise they would hardly have agreed to
run into debt. Therefore they were at the mercy of the Utopians
and altogether in their hands. More's answer to this would have been
that the Utopians were not interested in gaining power or making
profits and would therefore continue to act in a humane manner. But
why did they export if this was the case? Either they were urged on
by economic needs or—whether intentionally or not—by the desire
for economic or political power. What kind of politics was this when
one bought one's security by bribing foreign rulers with gold, caused
them to commit treachery against their own people or to fall out with
their neighbors: what, if not power politics?

However sincere our moralist, he had not evaded the demonic aspect
of power. The twilight penetrated into his assumed clarity. In certain
circumstances it appeared that the flourishing island might suffer from
being overpopulated. In that case their living space would become
insufficient. It would then be right to found colonies overseas wherever
there was an abundance of agricultural land. If the natives wanted

to live with the newcomers they would be allowed to merge with them. Those who refused to live in accordance with Utopian law would be expelled; and war would be waged against them since war was considered justified if the soil would not otherwise be used. It would be wrong to resist settlement and yet let the soil lie fallow. Oncken thought that More was referring to Ireland in this context; if so one may think that More's recommendations appear to have been followed by the English with regard to the Irish. In that case *Utopia* would stand at the beginning of the long series of state papers which justified British imperialism as it developed throughout the next centuries! Recent English research has shown that Thomas More personally participated in a colonial enterprise undertaken by his brother-in-law, John Rastell, six months after the publication of the book. They tried to found a British trading station on the shores of Newfoundland (which had been discovered a short time before by John Cabot) and to oust the French there from the trade in fish, timber, tar and pitch. This would indeed explain More's special interest in colonial enterprises. Should he have had in mind Newfoundland instead of Ireland, his words would not be burdened by the memory—which later generations cannot cast from their minds—of cruel suppression which crowded the stage. In any case, one must be careful not to transform More into an early prophet of British expansionism. This began several centuries later and could not have been foreseen either by him or by his contemporaries. Chambers rightly states that More did not claim any monopoly rights for his Utopians but recommended all European States to switch their urge of conquest from their neighbors to the empty spaces overseas.

It remained remarkable, however, that More thought of expansion on virgin soil not only as being less obnoxious, even if it involved war, than the continental kind of conquest, but as truly commendable and in accordance with the laws of nature. Like others amongst his contemporaries he was anxious to divert his monarch from useless adventures on the continent of Europe to overseas expeditions (which succeeded only once for a short while in 1521). Instinctively he appeared to share the view—which became general in England—that the European system alone was subject to the restrictions of international law of that time, while a new "freedom of the seas" ruled the wide open expanse of the ocean and the newly discovered western fringes of the continents beyond—only the natural law of pure force was valid in the territories overseas. Characteristically enough he could not speak of force without giving it some moral justification. He invented a law of nature which demanded that unused soil should not be allowed to lie fallow forever. Justice demanded that it was given to those who needed it, or thought they needed it. And whosoever resisted this just demand could justly expect war by way of punishment.

In the light of this, More's conception of the nature of power could be easily understood. His criticism of feudal society and medieval monarchies had for its starting-point the idea of social justice. And the same belief lay at the basis of his view of a just foreign policy. The use of the power of the State appeared to him, the legally trained man, morally justified only when it was a question of carrying out a legal judgment, or where it could be thought of in these terms of justice. Political struggle remained to him a struggle for legal right. The demonic character of power was hidden behind the mask of justice, and therefore remained outside the observer's ken. The Utopians who fought for power did not appear as promoters of their own cause but in the shape of judges: yet, viewed from the point of vantage supplied by Machiavelli's law of nature, this put them doubly in the wrong since they now appeared—in the eyes of the Machiavellian!— as deceitful and pharisaic, in fact like wolves in sheep's clothing.

Thomas More judged these facts quite differently. He took it for granted that the Utopians were morally and culturally superior to all their neighbors since the latter were not governed in accordance with the just principles of liberty. This was at the basis of all his considerations, moral and political. This led him to state, e.g., that the Utopians thought it right to free other nations from slavery. Out of gratitude for such liberation—or out of admiration—other countries asked the Utopians to lend them magistrates and officials who were to govern them either for terms of a single year or for periods of five years. More was convinced that strangers could not make a better choice; they could rely on utterly unselfish administrators from Utopia, on men who could not be bribed and would be invariably just. He also took it for granted that countries thus governed would always act as "friends" or "allies" of the island. It is not necessary to doubt the purity of his missionary zeal and yet to notice that such methods, applied in practice, would be indistinguishable from mere modern imperialism. Instead of oppression, it was friendship and alliances which led to economic and political dependency upon the island power; this, after all, was the natural road to power for any island State, the geographical position of which made difficult military conquest and occupation of foreign towns. This rendered the conclusion of formal alliances inadvisable since they would lead unnecessarily to foreign entanglements and strife. The Utopians therefore never entered into firm alliances but preferred a kind of splendid isolation; they knew that they were safe in their island anyway. But they used a moral argument in favor of this attitude: knowing how others broke their word continuously and how they perverted the meaning of treaties—these were, after all, the standard features of continental alliances—Utopia decided to hold itself aloof from such corruption (and More's irony found a fertile ground when he described contemporary treachery). Was not the community of all mankind and the well-being of all nations, a better guarantee of the peace than any bilateral agreement could ever be? Bilateral treaties always aimed at mutual deceit. Would not treaties lead to counter-treaties? Worse, did not nations consider one another as enemies unless they were formally bound to one another by a treaty?

Utopia, secure in the knowledge of its own moral superiority, also knew how to act in times of war. It would be wrong to think of More as an absolute pacifist like Erasmus. His Utopians underwent military training and thus followed the model set by Plato's republic or the description given by classical authors of teutonic bravery. When honor demanded otherwise it was despicable for a Utopian to cling to life. They arranged for training, e.g., by placing fiery horses at the disposal of their young men who were also taught to swim fully armed; they invented engines of war and even trained their womenfolk. If war penetrated into their own country, compulsory training was accepted and applied even to the coward. Only wars abroad were fought by a voluntary army. More described in great detail and with visible interest the technique employed by Utopians at war, leading up to an almost classical battle piece. The true strength of the front was not employed till late, and reserves were carefully husbanded so that victory was secure. Women fought at the front, each warrior being surrounded by his family, and nobody forsook anybody else. Priests spurred them on and asked for the blessing of their god. A troop of carefully picked young men struck again and again against the enemy's leader—the battle must be fought to its bloody end.

Obviously More was concerned with contrasting a battle which was fought by a whole nation, with the traditional methods of a feudal army where—stage-like—duels were fought. His own description breathed classical heroism and a determination surpassing even the radical plans Machiavelli had put forward for the arming of the citizens. All the more strange was More's attempt to rationalize warfare and to give to war, the most basic of all vital expressions of a State's wish for power, the appearance of an act of political humanity. It was only natural and sensible that he tried to restrict their occurrence, the passions roused and the horrors caused by wars; natural, too, that he tried to secure the rule of reason even in wartime. But he did not stop there. He could not grasp war in any other form than as an instrument of justice meting out punishment. To accept war in all innocence as a struggle of opposing Powers ordained by nature would have meant to confess that human reason and human morals were incapable of overcoming the chaotic contradictions involved in man's passionate desires. It would have been the abdication of reason and an acceptance of man's incapacity to produce harmony in this world. Indeed, Utopians would then have been reduced to the same level at which the other nations lived.

More's ideal Utopians detested war despite their military prowess and their readiness to defend, come what may, their own country. They thought war to be very beastly, and any thirst for military glories to be unworthy of man. Yet, unlike Erasmus, they recognized war to be just and necessary in certain cases. There was, e.g., the war to defend their own country, fought in principle outside their island by means of preventive action or by their own forces. Next, there was the war of assistance fought on behalf of friends who were threatened; the colonial war against natives who resisted foreign rule; and the war of liberation on behalf of the suppressed who suffered tyranny or slavery: the latter the Utopians assisted out of pure humanity, naturally expecting in exchange gratefulness and practical friendship. But they also fought wars of revenge on behalf of their friends if asked to do so, and if they approved of the reasons, especially in cases where the trade of their friends had severely suffered. They did not shun the shedding of much blood in order to secure the triumph or the domination of their friends over other nations. If they themselves had been slighted, they would be less ready to act, particularly if it had only meant loss of wealth, not loss of life. Economic sanctions, say trade boycott, might be resorted to; otherwise the handing over of the guilty (established by a Utopian ambassador) and punishment by death or slavery might be considered sufficient. Refusal to grant such demands would, however, cause an immediate declaration of war.

This list of justifiable wars was considerably longer than any drawn up by medieval writers, even if the theologians had generally restricted themselves to rather slight statements. More must have been anxious to make allowances for the newly found national pride of modern nations and, at the same time, to allow his rational aims to displace the dynastic views of knightly honor as formerly entertained by feudal rulers. The trading interests, the honor and the rights of every member of the community were to be of equal concern, or of even greater concern, to the State than any dynastic ambitions; for the latter, indeed, he left no room at all. But what did this mean if not the replacement of the dynastic interests of princes by the striving for power and position experienced by whole nations? Could one doubt that More, in doing this, had not opened the gate wide for imperialistic aims and for forces that urged Utopians on to gain power, and still more power?

Even more doubtful was More's attempt to humanize warfare by rationalizing it. He was concerned not so much with the prevention of bloodshed as such but with shedding less of the precious blood of Utopians, such highly educated and noble people! That is why they tried to defeat the enemy first by trickery, treachery and plotting. Only such victories won by intellectual prowess over brute animal force were commemorated by them in triumphal marches and statues —a feature that must be reckoned amongst the intentionally grotesque things in this satire. But how did they achieve their aim? Especially through propaganda abroad. Once war had begun they promised huge sums to anyone killing the enemy's ruler, further substantial sums to anyone disposing of leading enemy politicians, especially war-mongers. Double the sum was due to him who caught such an opponent alive. And the leaders thus declared outcasts were urged to take action against one another. Utopians caused misunderstanding, distrust and treachery throughout the enemy's camp. Their large treasure in gold enabled them to pay gigantic sums or to hand over large estates to traitors who could enjoy their gains in the safety of a friendly or neutral State.

More realized that his desire for humane methods of warfare which would reduce the loss of life had led him to recommend immoral actions. He expected resistance from all right-thinking people; and he really asked for this by overdoing it in the most grotesque manner. Yet, he pointed again and again to his humanitarian aims: better that a few died than that whole armies were slaughtered. Stubbornly he invented more daring details still. Any means and any method of Machiavellian craftiness appeared justified if it but shortened the war and brought it to a quick and triumphant end. If bribery proved of no avail, Utopians caused usurpers to put in a claim to the enemy's throne and made factions stake out new demands. They urged neighbors to rise and join in the war "under the color of some old title or right, such as kings never lack." Promising help and aid, they sent money continuously, but no soldiers as long as this could be avoided. If military help proved unavoidable the Utopians would hire soldiers anywhere in the world and send them to the front. Particularly useful for this service were the wild mountain tribes of the Zapoletes (More presumably thought of Swiss mercenaries). The Zapoletes were born only to war, were murderers whose death nobody could regret. They were used for the most dangerous work; the greater the number of Zapoletes killed, the better. "The Utopians care not how many of them they bring to destruction. For they believe that they should do a very good deed for all mankind, if they could rid out of the world all that foul stinking den of that most wicked and cursed people." More's strongest condemnation was indeed reserved for these warring tribes.

Next to these mercenaries the Utopians made use of the soldiers belonging to the country on whose behalf the war was fought; then of the armies of further friends; and only finally of Utopian soldiers themselves. Utopians counted for far too much to be risked except in cases of real emergency. Why indeed should one envisage the highly educated Utopian fighting the crude, uncouth mercenaries of the continental State! Utopians lived on a higher plane, and if they went to war they did so only on behalf of higher justice. Their wars were meant as punishment and the re-establishment of the law. It was only right, therefore, that the conquest of the enemy's town was followed by slavery for its defenders and by the strangling of the rebel leaders who had dragged out the fight—and by a handsome reward for those good citizens who had advised capitulation. Prisoners of war were turned into slaves or treated like other criminals; they had to do forced labor for Utopia (which was still better than the fate of prisoners at that time: then they were generally slaughtered). Finally, the vanquished paid heavy reparations; indeed, successful wars had made the Utopians one of the wealthiest of nations. Others paid them tribute, partly out of the revenue from big estates.

This completed the picture of Utopian power politics in peace and war. In order rightly to judge Thomas More the reader must recall, even if this appears difficult at times, that he spoke of an unreal dream island, not of England. It was not the conceit of a modern nationalist but the old-fashioned strictness of a true moralist which made him speak so harshly and ignobly of all non-Utopians. He simply did not see that in any given instance in history all the right is but rarely on one side—and this is so even in the fight of civilized man against the barbarian! Perhaps he can best be understood if the wars fought by Utopians are viewed quite literally as described, namely as wars between a highly civilized ("white") people and wild tribes of other continents. More, of course, did not think, even for a moment, of racial differences but exclusively of different levels of civilization and morality. The European of today who looks back on a long history of colonial expansion and whose political thinking, alas, tends to run along biological rather than moral lines, might perhaps be willing to apply More's contradistinction to "racially inferior" people of a lower standard, say in Central Africa, and even approve, without much reluctance, Utopian methods in such cases. Why should a person with such prejudices think Utopians conceited because they looked down upon their barbarian neighbors and refused to treat them as their equals? Probably just because he cannot help thinking of England when he should think of Utopia and of the European nations when he ought to accept More's description of the undeveloped neighbor States. More can be held responsible for this only in so far as he himself stressed similarities. It has caused some to see in him not an abstract moralist, preaching pure ethics, but a modern nationalist with an overdose of conceit.

One further fact must be mentioned in this context. Machiavelli had seen that the urge for power which, emerging as it does from the demonic twilight, knows no moral bounds whatsoever when it grips the addict of force. He had seen further than that. He had recognized that it could hold in its grip whole nations. It needed but a demagogue to permeate a whole people with the thirst for power and to make them break all barriers. Medieval thought about tyranny had known nothing about these demonic forces; nor had Erasmus. The ideals of a Christian government were preached exclusively for the benefit of the rulers themselves, and it was to them, to their conscience and humanity that these writers had appealed. Thomas More for his part followed them, and indeed helped to keep their view to the foreground for many more centuries, so that it continued to exert an influence throughout Europe. He took it for granted, and so did Erasmus, that military ambitions and the thirst for conquest were eternal vices of tyrants while a free people was peaceful and good neighborly. If this had been a stand-by of all medieval thought about tyranny, it was to become one of the most effective weapons of British propaganda. More was certain that his Utopians, as long as they lived as free men, would follow reason and morality in their dealings with other countries. This opened up a line of thought which led to the conception of a nation united in one State to which would be ascribed so high a moral value as to justify any use of power as long as it was applied in the name of that nation. The will of a freely united nation, and its strength, might then be used to hide the demonic nature of that power and to cover up the Machiavellian abuse of force on behalf of that nation.

Thomas More was far removed from any such development. All one can say is that even the peaceful welfare state of the Utopians stood revealed, at close inspection, as a State based on power. In its foreign policy one recognizes all those demonic features which More, the humanist, had tried, in all sincerity, to ban. He had hoped to do this by the application of a reasonable political and social order. However thick the veil of moral ideologies behind which the demonic Gorgon's head had been hidden, it remained there, an awful sight.

93073

And those who lift the veil are not less frightened than those who try to meet the direct stare of hard reality, namely those who trace the features of political reality as manfully and as frankly as did Machiavelli.

# The Bourgeois Point of View

## by Russell Ames

The social relations of More's time and his class position . . . set
the necessary framework within which such thought as his could
develop. And therefore, the main thesis of the present study may be
broadly stated thus: *Utopia* is not an accident of individual genius
but a product of capitalism's attack on feudalism, a part of middle-
class and humanist criticism of a decaying social order. From this it
follows that whatever More may have derived from Plato, Augustine,
and Thomas Aquinas, he is more significant to us as a precursor of
Diderot, Jefferson, and Sun Yat Sen. Though it is true that the
*Utopia* is somewhat anti-capitalist, both from an idealist-medieval
and an embryonic-socialist point of view, the core of the book is republican, bourgeois, and democratic—the result of More's experience
as a man of business, as a politician, and as an Erasmian reformer.

\* \* \*

More's *Utopia* expresses the various reforming purposes of the
statesman, the lawyer, the merchant, the humanist, and the man of
religion. These purposes were, of course, intertwined and overlapping
as well as distinguishable. The middle class, in its inconsistent and
only partly conscious campaign against feudalism, had the merchants
as its chief economic power and the humanists as its ideological shock
troops—with More active in both groups. The *Utopia,* incorporating
many views acceptable to the London merchants, presented a program
of social reform, and was, first of all, a humanist tract. Its form and
spirit owed much to classical literature and to religious tradition, but
its substance was contemporary and secular.

The hypothesis may be very seriously projected that the *Utopia*
in every detail had a practical meaning in More's day. This is not
to say that More was urging his contemporaries immediately to
institute in their societies every practice of the Utopians. The hypoth-

*From Russell Ames,* Citizen Thomas More and His Utopia *(Princeton, N. J.:
Princeton University Press, 1949), excerpted from the Introduction, pp. 6–13. Reprinted by permission of the publisher.*

esis implies, rather, that those Utopian practices which were fantastic consistently indicated a practical line of conduct which would be understood by sympathetic readers.

R. W. Chambers, in the most notable of recent books on More, shows that many Utopian customs and ordinances directly reflect More's opinions of current problems, particularly religious problems. Chambers believes, however, that More often makes his Utopians do things which are not approved because the Utopians follow reason rather than the imperatives of the Christian religion. It is more accurate to say that even when the Utopians depart from practices acceptable to Christianity, they do so in such a way as to indicate how a sixteenth century European should behave. Chambers feels that "The underlying thought of *Utopia* always is, *With nothing save Reason to guide them, the Utopians do this; and yet we Christian Englishmen, we Christian Europeans . . . !*" This is certainly part of the meaning of Utopia; but it may be better phrased thus: *The Utopians, guided by Reason and also by their basically sound religion, have almost achieved a truly Christian ideal which they live by while we Christians do not.* In short, though More was limited by the necessities of keeping his fiction logical, consistent, and an adequate disguise for his attacks and proposals, he makes every effort within this framework to teach social and religious truth. The Utopians "joine unto the reasons of Philosophye certeyne principles taken oute of religion: wythoute the whyche . . . they thynke reason of it selfe weake and unperfecte." The Utopians have more than reason to guide them, and are quite conscious of the fact; their only real difference from Europeans is that they actually follow reason, which leads them closer and closer to Christian religion and to ideal Christian behavior.[1]

The hypothesis outlined above suggests the following type of analysis. Utopian children confess their misdeeds to their parents. This does not mean that More advises English children to stop confessing to priests. It means two quite different things: first, the Utopians, though not in contact with Christianity, by reason and natural religion found their way to confession, and this proves that the confessional as ordained by the church is both a godly and a rational institution; secondly, the Utopian practice suggests that a virtuous Utopian parent is a better confessor than a corrupt European priest, and that the latter had better reform himself. Thus, the institution of confession is upheld, and at the same time reform is advocated. Similarly, when we see that in *Utopia* many religions are permitted, we should not assume that More advocates the dismemberment of European Christianity and the

---

[1] Budé wrote that the Utopians "have adopted Christian usages both in public and in private." (Quoted in J. H. Lupton, ed., *Utopia* [Oxford: at the Clarendon Press, 1895], lxxxvii.)

institution of many new religions. More does mean, however, in these years before Luther appeared on his horizon, that true faith will peacefully conquer false ideas, that bigoted repressions may halt that revival of true religion which Colet and Erasmus were attempting, and that it is unchristian for Portuguese gold-hunters to drive Indians into church with the sword. More's general discussion of religion in Utopia is meant to prove, not the superiority of agnosticism to Christianity, but that Christianity has nothing to fear from peace, freedom, and rational criticism.

The meaning of More's apparent advocacy of communism—a question more closely related to the main interest of this study—can be understood through a similar type of analysis. It is improbable, though possible, that More was a practical advocate of communism in England, however much he *may* have been drawn to the theory of it. The lesson of Utopian communism is, however, that economic conditions are the cause of social evils and that the English ruling classes will not make themselves happier and wealthier by overworking, dispossessing, hanging, or failing to employ the poor, or even by exhorting the poor with pious phrases to a better life. In such futile ways they will only impoverish their country. Instead, they must revive husbandry and clothworking, improve law and government, and extend trade. Most critics of *Utopia* have spent so much time trying to prove either that communism won't work, or that More was not a communist, that they have ignored the immediate and practical significance of his economic criticism.

Many other aspects of the *Utopia* need detailed rather than abstract attention. More the lawyer, as well as More the saint, the humanist, and the statesman, wrote the book. His actual practice as a lawyer clearly led him to the severest criticism of legal trickery and injustice. His legal studies, however, probably gave him part of his social ideals. The Roman law, to which he had some attachment as a member of a society of Roman lawyers, did support the claims of absolute monarchy, but it also, in the Justinian code, proposed a harmonious commonwealth of nations which was an ideal of More's both in Utopia and in England. John Rastell, More's brother-in-law, in his preface to a *Book of Assizes* which he printed in 1513, praises the function of good laws as a curb upon greed: "Wealth, power and glory are . . . in themselves evil things, since they cannot be achieved except at the cost of impoverishment, subjection and humiliation. They cannot, for that reason, constitute the commonweal."

Similarly, the influence of primitive Christian communism on *Utopia* has not been emphasized, though *Utopia* itself emphasizes it. The direct effect of the Gospels must have been strong. Even more important was the republican, and more or less radical economic character of northern humanism. From this, which is not the main subject of the present study, probably flows the major influence on *Utopia*.

That the first book refers in a general way to contemporary social evils is, of course, obvious to all readers. That the whole work refers frequently to specific events with which More was often personally acquainted, is not so well known.

Some of the more obvious examples can show how specific these references were. Hythloday, telling why he will not take service as an adviser to princes, asked More how the king of France would respond if advised to govern his own land well and give up foreign invasion, and More admitted that the king would not be pleased with the advice. This is no general, classical attack on war but a definite reference to the invasion of Italy by Francis I in the preceding year (1515) which culminated in the victory of Marignano in September. Clearly the advice against invasion applied equally well to Henry VIII's invasions of France (1512–1514). Hythloday's description of the way kings are advised to get money perfectly describes the recent practices of Henry VII: juggling the value of currency, feigning war and taxing for it, reviving old laws to collect new fines, establishing new regulations to sell exemption from them. Particularly, the attack on the revival of old Crown privileges points to Henry VII's collection of dues for the knighting of his dead son Arthur, which More resisted in the parliament of 1504. It was noted above that shafts directed against Francis I also struck Henry VIII: similarly criticism of Henry VII applied in part to Henry VIII. Both the French and the Utopian practice of bribing and corrupting enemy populations suggested the intrigues of Henry VIII and his minister Dacre, who sowed treason among the Scotch lords. It is reasonable to assume that every item of criticism in *Utopia* recalled to well-informed readers precise events in current history, many of which may not be easy to identify today.

More's connections with the merchants of London, with the Court, and with humanists, kept him familiar also with more remote continental affairs and even with some African, Asian, and American conditions. Reports at this time from Sir Robert Wingfield, English ambassador to the Emperor Maximilian, are rich in references to the politics of eastern Europe, the Turkish threat, and Italian conditions. The direct attack on international intrigues in the first book of *Utopia*, as well as the ironic attack in the second book, were unusually apropos in these two years (1515–1516) when the book was being written. International relations were peculiarly unstable. Peace had just come in 1514 after England's successful wars against France. In 1515 France invaded Italy and won an unexpected victory which sharply changed the balance of forces. The new peace following was of the most fluid character, and the diplomatic correspondence of the time shows that all cats were ready to jump in any direction at any moment.

The influence of foreign events and conditions on Utopia has hardly been mentioned by its students, though Chambers discusses the problem of the unity of Christendom against the Turk, and points out, concerning More's embassy of 1515, that "Everywhere in *Utopia* we can trace the influence of these [Flemish] foreign scholars and foreign men of affairs, as well as of the civilization of the noble Flemish cities." This was probably the most important continental influence, for More did not travel much elsewhere. It is noted by J. H. Lupton, who contrasts London with the towns of Flanders.

Also important among the influences on *Utopia* were ideals of city and guild life, and a popular English devotion to the commonweal. It is surprising that Kautsky, a socialist, neglects these, though he pays general tribute to the liberty-loving sentiments of the English and emphasizes his belief that More, in peculiar English conditions, differed from other humanists in his concern for the people. The youthful radicalism of John Rastell, More's brother-in-law, and his ideal of the commonwealth expressed in legal theory, the common weal advocated by economists like Clement Armstrong—all these . . . are native parallels to *Utopia,* and express its practical content, rather than its literary form as Plato's *Republic* does.

To summarize the problem of the general character of *Utopia:* rather abstract polemics over religion and communism, divorced from the detailed events of More's experience, have obscured *Utopia*'s nature as an effort at practical social reform.

# A Sermon on Pride

## by J. H. Hexter

. . . The Utopian economy does not justify itself as modern economies do by claiming to give men in the fullest measure the things they
want; it is not based on the tacit assumption of modern economies that
on the whole what men want is what they ought to have. The shadow
of Bentham lies forward over Mill and Marx, Kautsky and Keynes—it
does not fall backward over More. The justification for the Utopian
system in all its aspects, economic and other, is that it provides all men
with what they need in the measure that they need it; and while men
ought to have what they need, they certainly do not need and ought
not to have in full, or any other measure, whatever they happen to
want. In *Utopia* there is no touch of the Benthamite doctrine that
pushpin is as good as poetry, or better if more people want it. More
not only limits the wants which the Good Society ought to satisfy;
he also sets a ceiling on the quality and kinds of goods that properly
may be produced to satisfy even those legitimate wants. What appear
to be the economic institutions of Utopia—community of property,
abolition of markets and money—are economic in form but not in
purpose. Their strictly economic function is incidental. In More's
eyes, as we shall see, they serve not economic but other and higher
ends.

We are better equipped to discover what those ends are now that we
know that bond labor, abolition of markets and money, and restriction
of wants by enforced community of consumption are of a piece with
the abolition of private property and profit and with the obligation
to toil—indispensable motifs in the total pattern of More's best state
of the commonwealth. A society where wants are tightly bound up
and where the penal power of the state is made daily conspicuous by
men in heavy gold chains—this is no ideal society of Modern Socialism.
Altogether missing from *Utopia* is that happy anarchist last chapter

---

*From J. H. Hexter, "The Roots of* Utopia *and All Evil," in* More's *Utopia:* The
Biography of an Idea *(Princeton, N. J.: Princeton University Press, 1952), pp. 70–81.
Copyright © 1952 by Princeton University Press. Reprinted by permission of the
publisher.*

of modern socialism intended to justify all the struggle, all the suffering, all the constraint that we must undergo in order to reach it. *Utopia* does not end in an eschatological dream.

More simply did not believe that all the evil men do can be ascribed to the economic arrangements of society, and that those evils and the very potentiality for evil will vanish when the economic arrangements are rectified and set on a proper footing. More believed no such thing because in his view of men and their affairs there was a strong and ineradicable streak of pessimism. More's pessimism was ineradicable because it was part and parcel of his Christian faith. He knew surely, as a profoundly Christian man he had to know, that the roots of evil run far too deep in men to be destroyed by a mere rearrangement of the economic organization of society. His residue of pessimism leads More to provide even "the best state of the commonwealth" with an elaborate complement of laws drastically limiting the scope given to individual human desires and to arm its government with extensive and permanent powers of coercion. Although he was convinced that the institutions of the society that he knew provided the occasions for the evils he saw, he did not—and as a profoundly orthodox Christian he could not—believe that the evils were totally ascribable to the institutions. His probings led him to believe that the roots of the evils of sixteenth century Europe, though nourished in the rich black earth of an acquisitive society, were moistened by the inexhaustible stream of sin.

Underlying the whole catalogue of evils of his time he finds one or another of several sins. Luxury, gluttony, envy, vanity, vainglory, lust, hypocrisy, debauchery, sloth, bad faith and the rest all find an easy vent in the Christendom he knew, whose institutions seemed to him as if contrived to activate human wickedness and anesthetize human decency. Yet More does not give equal attention to all the kinds of sin; the realm of evil is not a republic of equals. The Deadly Sins themselves are not on an even footing in the Utopian Discourse. Gluttony and Anger get short shrift, Envy is there only as a counterfoil to a deadlier sin, and Lust, that whipping boy of our feeble latter-day Christianity, receives but a passing glance. The great triumvirate that rules the empire of evil, are Sloth, Greed, and Pride.

It is sloth that in More's day leads stout fellows able to work to enter into the idle bands of serving men; it is sloth that leads them to fill with drinking, gaming, and brawling the hours they ought to spend in honest toil. It is sloth, the avoidance of labor, that the Utopians punish with bondage. Yet although to More's mind idleness was among the most destructive cankers on the social body, although it preoccupied him as much as any other problem, he did not blame that idleness wholly on sloth. The lazy good-for-nothing scum that the great leave in their wake is conjured into being by the great men themselves, who provide their followers with the means of debauchery and vice. And it is not sloth but a greater sin that leads the great men to foster the infection of idleness in the body of the commonwealth.

Even above sloth in the hierarchy of sin lie greed and pride. In dealing with these two paramount sins More's Christian faith stood him in good stead. It provided him with a basic insight into the underlying pattern of evil, a pattern somewhat obscured by our modern climate of opinion. For he did not believe that greed and pride were on a parity with each other as sources of the social ills of his day, or that they offered equal obstacles to the establishment of the Good Society; but at this point it requires special care to read More's meaning right. The best known passage of *Utopia,* the attack on enclosure in the Dialogue section [Book I], is directed against the "inordinate and insatiable covetousness" of landlords and engrossers. Much of the Discourse section [Book II], moreover, is taken up with variation after variation on a single theme: "The love of money is the root of all evil." Now the inordinate desire for riches is greed or avarice, and from this it would seem to follow almost as a syllogism that greed was what More discovered as a result of his social analysis to be the fount and origin of the sickness of his own society. Yet it is not so. Greed was a sin, revolting enough in More's eyes; but it is not a sufficiently attractive vice to stand alone. Men are impelled to it not by its charms, but, like other animals, by fear of want. *"Why,"* Hythloday asks, *"should anyone consider seeking superfluities, when he is certain that he will never lack anything? Indeed in all kinds of living things it is . . . fear of want that creates greed and rapacity."* It is one of the perverse traits of the regime of private property, where each must make provision for and look after his own, that an amiable regard for his kin continually tempts man to the sin of avarice.

But this sin, certain to beset a pecuniary society, is essentially a parasite on the insecurity inherent in that kind of society and has no roots of its own. It is sustained rather by the institutional roots of the property system itself. Even the rich, More suggests, realize this, and are "not ignorant how much better it were to lack no necessary thing than to abound with overmuch superfluity, to be rid out of innumerable cares and troubles, than to be *bound down*[1] by great riches." If avarice were the great danger to society the Utopian commonwealth could be instituted along lines far less rigorous and repressive than those More prescribes. But avarice is not all. Fear of want makes for greed in all living creatures, including man; in man alone

---

[1] "be besieged with"; *obsideri.*

greed has a second set of roots deeper in his nature even than fear. For men only of God's creatures are greedy out of "pride alone, which counts it a glorious thing to pass and excel others in the superfluous and vain ostentation of things." Here, I think, lies the heart of the matter. Deep in the soul of the society of More's day, because it was deep in the soul of all men, was the monster Pride, distilling its terrible poison and dispatching it to all parts of the social body to corrupt, debilitate, and destroy them. Take but a single example: Why must the poor in Europe be "wearied from early in the morning to late in the evening with continual work like laboring and toiling beasts" leading a life "worse than the miserable and wretched condition of bondmen, which nevertheless is almost everywhere the life of workmen and artificers?" Human beings are consigned to this outrageous slavery merely to support the enormous mass of the idle, and to perform the "vain and superfluous" work that serves "only for riotous superfluity and unhonest pleasure." What feeds the unhonest pleasure that men derive from luxuries and vanities, or to use the phrase of a modern moralist, from conspicuous consumption and conspicuous waste? It is pride. Many men drudge out their lives making vain and needless things because other men "count themselves nobler for the smaller or finer thread of wool" their garb is made of, because "they think the *value*[2] of their own persons is thereby greatly increased. And therefore the honor, which in a coarse gown they dare not have looked for, they require, as it were of duty, for their finer gowns' sake. And if they be passed by without reverence, they take it angrily and disdainfully." The same sickness of soul shows itself in "pride in vain and unprofitable honors." "For what natural or true pleasure doest thou take of another man's bare head or bowed knees? Will this ease the pain of thy knees or remedy the frenzy of thy head? In this image of counterfeit pleasure they be of a marvelous madness *who flatter and applaud themselves with the notion of their own nobility*." [3] It is to support this prideful and conceited "opinion of nobility" that men must be treated like beasts of burden to keep idlers in luxury. The great mass of wastrels bearing down on Christendom are maintained to minister to the pride and vainglory of the great. Such are "the flock of stout bragging rushbucklers," "the great . . . train of idle and loitering servingmen," that "rich men, especially all landed men, which commonly be called gentlemen and noblemen," themselves fainéants, "carry about with them at their tails." Such too are the armies, maintained by those paragons of pride, the princes of Europe, out of the

[2] "price"; *precii*.
[3] "which for the opinion of nobility rejoice much in their own conceit"; *ii qui nobilitatis opinione sibi blandiuntur ac plaudunt.*

blood and sweat of their subjects, to sustain their schemes of megalo-
maniac self-glorification. Thus seeking in outward, vain, and wicked
things an earthly worship which neither their achievement nor their
inner virtue warrants, Christians lure their fellow men into the sin of
sloth, or subject them to endless labor, or destroy their substance, their
bodies, and their souls too, in futile wars; and over the waste and the
misery, over the physical ruin and the spiritual, broods the monster
sin of pride.

The Utopian Discourse then is based on a diagnosis of the ills of
sixteenth century Christendom; it ascribes those ills to sin, and primarily to pride, and it prescribes remedies for that last most disastrous
infection of man's soul designed to inhibit if not to eradicate it. For
our understanding of the Utopian Discourse it is of the utmost importance that we recognize this to be its theme. Unless we recognize it,
we cannot rescue More from the ideologically motivated scholars of the
Left and the Right, both as anxious to capture him for their own as
if he were a key constituency in a close Parliamentary election. According to the Rightist scholars, who have allowed their nostalgia for an
imaginary medieval unity to impede their critical perceptions, More
was one of the last medieval men. He was the staunch defender of
Catholic solidarism represented in medieval order and liberties, in a
stable, agrarian subsistence economy, in guild brotherhood, monastic
brotherhood, and Christian brotherhood against the inchoate growth
of modern universal otherhood, already embodied, or shortly to be
embodied in nascent capitalism, the New Monarchy, Protestantism,
and Machiavellianism [R. W. Chambers; see above, pp. 17–32]. On
the other hand, the most recent exponent of the *Utopia* as an exem-
plification of dialectical materialism [Russell Ames; see above, pp.
53–57] has seen More as a fine early example of the Middle Class Man
whose social views are one and all colored by his antipathy to late
medieval feudalism as represented in the enfeebled but still exploitative
Church and in the predatory and decadent feudal aristocracy, making
their final rally in the courts of equally predatory and decadent dynastic warrior princes.

Both of these formulations—that of the Left and that of the Right
—are subject to a number of weaknesses. They are both based on
conceptions of economic development and social stratification in the
sixteenth century and earlier more coherent than correct, and largely
mythological in many respects. The Leftist scholars by regarding More's
age from a particular twentieth century perspective, the Rightists by
regarding it from what they fondly imagine to be a medieval perspective deprive both More's opinions and his age of the measure of internal cohesion that both in truth possess. But to document these
criticisms adequately would require an inordinate amount of space.

For the moment it must suffice to point out that from *Utopia* and from the events of More's life, scholarly ideologues both of the Left and of the Right have been able to adduce a remarkable number of citations and facts to support their respective and totally irreconcilable views. Now this paradox is amenable to one of two possible explanations. The first would require us to assume that More's thought was so contradictory, disorderly, and illogical as to justify either of these interpretations or both, although in reason and common sense they are mutually contradictory. But the intellectual coherence and sureness of thought of the Utopian Discourse and the sense of clear purpose that it radiates seem to preclude this resolution of the paradox. The second possibility is that either point of view can be maintained only by an unconscious but unjustifiable underestimate of the weight of the citations and data offered in support of the opposite point of view, but that all the citations and data fall into a harmonious pattern if looked at in a third perspective.

The character of that third possible perspective I have tried to suggest: the Utopian Discourse is the production of a Christian human-ist uniquely endowed with a statesman's eye and mind, a broad worldly experience, and a conscience of unusual sensitivity, who saw sin and especially the sin of pride as the cancer of the commonwealth. Now the social critic of any age is bound to direct his most vigorous attack at the centers of power in that age and reserve his sharpest shafts for the men possessing it. For however great the potentialities for evil may be in all men, real present social ills, the social critic's stock in trade, are immediately the consequence of the acts and decisions of the men actually in a position to inflict their wills on the social body. In a pecuniary society enjoying a reasonable measure of internal secur-ity and order but subject to great disparities of wealth, the social critic is bound to attack the very rich, because in such a society, where direct violence does not bear all the sway, riches become a most important source of power. This does not necessarily imply that pride is wholly confined to rich and powerful men, although by their possession of and preoccupation with money and power, the two goods most highly prized by the worldly, they are sure to be especially vulnerable to that sin. It is more to the point, however, that the pride of the powerful is, by virtue of their power, socially efficacious, since it is armed with the puissance of command. It can get what it wickedly wants. In More's Europe—the illicit violence of lordship almost everywhere having been suppressed by the new monarchs—it was the pride of the rich that did the real wicked work in the world, the work of fraud, oppres-sion, debauchery, waste, rapine, and death. So More's shafts find their target in the rich and the powerful—in the bourgeois usurer, the engrosser, the court minion, the mighty lord of lands and men, the

princes of the earth, in the encloser and depopulator whether that
encloser was a parvenu grazier-butcher still reeking of the blood of
the City shambles or a predacious noble of immaculate lineage or an
ancient abbey rich in estates and poor in things of the spirit. These
were his target not because together they form a homogeneous social
class, for they do not, nor because they are all decadently medieval or
all inchoately modern, for they are not all one or all the other, but
because their riches and power sustained the empire of pride over
the world that More knew and whose social ills he had traced to
that center of evils.

Once we recognize that More's analysis of sixteenth century society
led him to the conclusion that pride was the source of the greater
part of its ills, the pattern of the Utopian commonwealth becomes
clear, consistent, and intelligible. In its fundamental structure it is a
great social instrument for the subjugation of pride. The pecuniary
economy must be destroyed because money is the prime instrument
through the use of which men seek to satisfy their yet insatiable pride.
It is to keep pride down that all Utopians must eat in common messes,
wear a common uniform habit, receive a common education, and
rotate their dwelling places. In a society where no man is permitted
to own the superfluities that are the marks of invidious distinction,
no man will covet them. Above all idleness, the great emblem of pride
in the society of More's time, a sure mark to elevate the aristocrat
above the vulgar, is utterly destroyed by the common obligation of
common daily toil. It is through no accident, through no backwardness
of the Tudor economy, that More makes the Utopian commonwealth
a land austere and rigorous beyond most of the imaginary societies
elaborated by his later imitators. Had he cared only to consider man's
material welfare, his creature comfort, it need not have been so. More
was a logical man; he knew that to bind up pride on all sides it takes
a strait prison, and he did not flinch from the consequences of his
diagnosis. As he truly says this "kind of vice among the Utopians can
have no place."

Since More does not explicitly speak of pride very often in *Utopia*,
my emphasis on its role in his social thought on both the critical and
constructive side may seem exaggerated. Let anyone who thinks this
is so consider the words with which More draws Hythloday's peroration and the whole Discourse of the best state of a commonwealth to
its conclusion: "I doubt not that the respect of every man's private
commodity or else the authority of our Saviour Christ . . . would
have brought all the world long ago into the laws of this weal public,
if it were not that one only beast, the princess and mother of all mischief, Pride, doth withstand and let it. She measureth not wealth
and prosperity by her own commodities but by the miseries and incom-

modities of others; she would not by her good will be made a goddess if there were no wretches left *over whom she might, like a scornful lady, rule and triumph,*[4] over whose miseries her felicity might shine, whose poverty she might vex, torment, and increase by gorgeously setting forth her riches. This hellhound creeps into men's hearts; and plucks them back from entering the right path of life, and is so deeply rooted in men's breasts that she cannot be plucked out."

The disciplining of pride, then, is the foundation of the best state of the commonwealth. And more than that, it is pride itself that prevents actual realms from attaining to that best state.

[4] "whom she might be lady over to mock and scorn"; *quibus imperare atque insultare possit.*

# A Play of Wit

## by C. S. Lewis

. . . All seem to be agreed that [*Utopia*] is a great book, but hardly
any two agree as to its real significance: we approach it through a
cloud of contradictory eulogies. In such a state of affairs a good,
though not a certain, clue is the opinion of those who lived nearer
the author's time than we. Our starting-point is that Erasmus speaks
of it as if it were primarily a comic book; Tyndale despises it as
"poetry"; for Harpsfield it is a "iollye inuention," "pleasantly" set
forth; More himself in later life classes it and the *Praise of Folly*
together as books fitter to be burned than translated in an age prone
to misconstruction; Thomas Wilson, fifty years later, mentions it for
praise among "feined narrations and wittie invented matters (as though
they were true indeed)." This is not the language in which friend or
enemy or author (when the author is so honest a man as More) refer
to a serious philosophical treatise. It all sounds as if we had to do with
a book whose real place is not in the history of political thought so
much as in that of fiction and satire. It is, of course, possible that
More's sixteenth-century readers, and More himself, were mistaken.
But it is at least equally possible that the mistake lies with those
modern readers who take the book *au grand sérieux*. There is a cause
specially predisposing them to error in such a matter. They live in a
revolutionary age, an age in which modern weapons and the modern
revolutionary technique have made it only too easy to produce in the
real world states recognizably like those we invent on paper: writing
Utopias is now a serious matter. In More's time, or Campanella's, or
Bacon's, there was no real hope or fear that the paper states could be
"drawn into practice": the man engaged in blowing such bubbles
did not need to talk as if he were on his oath. And here we have to
do with one who, as the Messenger told him in the *Dialogue*, "used
to look so sadly" when he jested that many were deceived.

The *Utopia* has its serious, even its tragic, elements. It is, as its

From C. S. Lewis, English Literature in the Sixteenth Century Excluding Drama,
Vol. III of The Oxford History of English Literature (*Oxford: The Clarendon Press,*
*1954*), *167–71. Reprinted by permission of the publisher.*

translator Robynson says, "fruitful and profitable." But it is not a consistently serious philosophical treatise, and all attempts to treat it as such break down sooner or later. The interpretation which breaks down soonest is the "liberal" interpretation. There is nothing in the book on which the later More, the heretic-hunter, need have turned his back. There is no freedom of speech in Utopia. There is nothing liberal in Utopia. From it, as from all other imaginary states, liberty is more successfully banished than the real world, even at its worst, allows. The very charm of these paper citizens is that they cannot in any way resist their author: every man is a dictator in his own book. It is not love of liberty that makes men write Utopias. Nor does the *Utopia* give any color to Tyndale's view that More "knew the truth" of Protestantism and forsook it: the religious orders of the Utopians and their very temples are modelled on the old religion. On the other hand, it is not a defense of that old order against current criticisms; it supports those criticisms by choosing an abbot as its specimen of the bad landlord and making a friar its most contemptible character. R. W. Chambers, with whom died so much that was sweetest and strongest in English scholarship, advanced a much more plausible view. According to him the Utopians represent the natural virtues working at their ideal best in isolation from the theological; it will be remembered that they hold their Natural Religion only provisionally "onles any godlier be inspired into man from heuen." Yet even this leaves some features unaccounted for. It is doubtful whether More would have regarded euthanasia for incurables and the assassination of hostile princes as things contained in the Law of Nature. And it is very strange that he should make Hedonism the philosophy of the Utopians. Epicurus was not regarded by most Christians as the highest example of the natural light. The truth surely is that as long as we take the *Utopia* for a philosophical treatise it will "give" wherever we lean our weight. It is, to begin with, a dialogue: and we cannot be certain which of the speakers, if any, represents More's considered opinion. When Hythloday explains why his philosophy would be useless in the courts of kings More replies that there is "another philosophy more ciuil" and expounds this less intransigent wisdom so sympathetically that we think we have caught the very More at last; but when I have read Hythloday's retort I am all at sea again. It is even very doubtful what More thought of communism as a practical proposal. We have already had to remind ourselves, when considering Colet, that the traditional admission of communism as the law of uncorrupted Nature need carry with it no consequences in the world of practical sociology. It is certain that in the *Confutation* (1532) More had come to include communism among the "horrible heresies" of the Anabaptists and in the *Dialogue of Comfort* he defends private riches. Those who think of More as a "lost leader" may discount these later utterances. Yet even at the end of the *Utopia* he rejects the Utopian economics as a thing "founded of no good reason." The magnificent rebuke of all existing societies which precedes this may suggest that the rejection is ironical. On the other hand, it may mean that the whole book is only a satiric glass to reveal our own avarice by contrast and is not meant to give us directly practical advice.

These puzzles may give the impression that the *Utopia* is a confused book: and if it were intended as a serious treatise it would be very confused indeed. On my view, however, it appears confused only so long as we are trying to get out of it what it never intended to give. It becomes intelligible and delightful as soon as we take it for what it is—a holiday work, a spontaneous overflow of intellectual high spirits, a revel of debate, paradox, comedy and (above all) of invention, which starts many hares and kills none. It is written by More the translator of Lucian and friend of Erasmus, not More the chancellor or the ascetic. Its place on our shelves is close to *Gulliver* and *Erewhon*, within reasonable distance of Rabelais, a long way from the *Republic* or *New Worlds for Old*. The invention (the "poetry" of which More was accused) is quite as important as the merits of the polity described, and different parts of that polity are on very different levels of seriousness.

Not to recognize this is to do More grave injustice. Thus the suggestion that the acquisitive impulse should be mortified by using gold for purposes of dishonor is infantile if we take it as a practical proposal. If gold in Utopia were plentiful enough to be so used, gold in Utopia would not be a precious metal. But if it is taken simply as satiric invention leading up to the story of the child and the ambassadors, it is delicious. The slow beginning of the tale, luring us on from London to Bruges, from Bruges to Antwerp, and thence by reported speech to fabulous lands beyond the line, has no place in the history of political philosophy: in the history of prose fiction it has a very high place indeed. Hythloday himself, as we first see him, has something of the arresting quality of the Ancient Mariner. The dialogue is admirably managed. Mere conversation holds us contented for the first book and includes that analysis of the contemporary English situation which is the most serious and the most truly political part of the *Utopia*. In the second book More gives his imagination free rein. There is a thread of serious thought running through it, an abundance of daring suggestions, several back-handed blows at European institutions, and, finally, the magnificent peroration. But he does not keep our noses to the grindstone. He says many things for the fun of them, surrendering himself to the sheer pleasure of imagined geography, imagined language, and imagined institutions. That is what readers whose interests are rigidly political do not understand: but everyone who has ever made an imaginary map responds at once.

Tyndale's belief that More "knew the truth and forsook it" is a crude form of the error which finds in the *Utopia* a liberalism inconsistent with More's later career. There is no inconsistency. More was from the first a very orthodox Papist, even an ascetic with a hankering for the monastic life. At the same time it is true that the *Utopia* stands apart from all his other works. Religiously and politically he was consistent: but this is not to say that he did not undergo a gradual and honorable change very like that which overtook Burke and Wordsworth and other friends of liberty as the Revolutionary age began to show its true features. The times altered; and things that would once have seemed to him permissible or even salutary audacities came to seem to him dangerous. That was why he would not then wish to see the *Utopia* translated. In the same way any of us might now make criticisms of democracy which we would not repeat in the hour of its danger. And from the literary point of view there is an even greater gulf between the *Utopia* and the works which followed. It is, to speak simply, beyond comparison better than they.

# Utopian Felicity

## by Edward Surtz, S. J.

The Utopians "determine other all or the chiefest part of man's felicity [*felicitas*] to rest" in pleasure (*uoluptas*). But only the person who denies the immortality of the soul, the providence of God, and a future reward or punishment, would try, if he were thoroughly logical, to achieve pleasure "by right or wrong" (*per fas ac nefas*). The Utopians, conceding these three truths, do not hold that man's happiness lies in every sort of pleasure, but insist upon a certain kind of pleasure. Like Socrates, they deny that pleasures "are all alike and to be equally esteemed" and assert "that some pleasures arise from honorable and good desires, and others from those that are base, and that we ought to practise and esteem the one and control and subdue the other." The qualifications which they demand for the proper kind of pleasure are four in number, of which one is positive and three are negative.

First of all, happiness resides "only in that pleasure that is good and honest" (*bona atque honesta*). The Utopians insist that true pleasures are "good and honest" by *nature*. This is the *positive* norm. "Pleasure they call every motion or state of the body or mind wherein man hath naturally [*natura duce*] delectation." There are many things which are considered pleasurable, yet "which of their own nature [*suapte natura*] contain no pleasantness," and which have "no natural pleasantness in them" (*natura nihil insit suaue*). Some people, for example, foolishly think that a gown of fine thread surpasses one of coarse thread "by nature, and not by their mistaking" (*natura non errore*). Every pleasure, therefore, is good or bad by *nature* and will remain so forever. "No man's judgment, depraved and corrupt other by sickness or by custom, can change the nature of pleasure, more than it can do the nature of other things." It does not lie within the power of men "to change the things as they do the names of things."

How is one to determine practically and concretely the *natural* goodness or badness of a particular pleasure? One can solve every problem

*From Edward Surtz, S. J., "Criteria of True and False Pleasure," in* The Praise of Pleasure: Philosophy, Education, and Communism in More's *Utopia* (*Cambridge, Mass.: Harvard University Press, 1957*), *pp. 36–43. Copyright* © *1957 by the President and Fellows of Harvard College. Reprinted by permission of the publisher.*

by an application of the three negative norms. Only that object can be pleasurable by *nature* which does not involve (1) the loss of a greater pleasure, or (2) consequent pain and sorrow, or (3) injury to one's neighbor. These ill consequences "they think to follow of necessity, if the pleasure be unhonest" (*quod necessario sequi censent, si inhonesta sit*). Hence, they hold "no kind of pleasure forbidden whereof cometh no harm" (*ex quo nihil sequatur incommodi*). Of the three negative norms, the first two are of special importance and value to the individual; the third, to society.

In Hythloday's account the first two negative norms are linked together on the three occasions when they are mentioned. For example, the Utopians use in all things this precaution "that a less pleasure hinder not a bigger and that the pleasure be no cause of displeasure" (*neu dolorem aliquando uoluptas pariat*). In this respect the Utopians follow the same principle as the man who disbelieves in the three fundamental truths and who, by a perfectly logical conclusion, would "do all his diligence and endeavor to obtain pleasure by right or wrong, only avoiding this inconvenience, that the less pleasure should not be a let or hindrance to the bigger, or that he labored not for that pleasure which would bring after it displeasure, grief, and sorrow" (*eam . . . quam inuicem retaliet dolor*). This latter statement accords with the assertion of Torquatus the Epicurean in Cicero's *De Finibus:* "The wise man . . . always holds . . . to the principle of selection: he rejects pleasures to secure other greater pleasures, or else he endures pains to avoid worse pains." Many years after the *Utopia* was published, More was to enunciate in his *Dialogue Concerning Heresies* a like principle of selection in speaking of the subordination of body to soul: "Wherein God would that we were learned rather to suffer our sensual parties plain and mourn than to follow their own hurt and ours too."

The third negative norm is social in character. It is directed with special force against the masters of England and Europe: the "conspiracy of rich men, procuring their own commodities under the name and title of the commonwealth." The Utopians derive their argument from nature herself. Nature does not lavish special attention and devotion upon any particular individual as though he did not belong to the mass of humanity but stood above it as a superman: "no man is so far above the lot of man's state or condition that nature doth cark and care for him only." On the contrary, nature "equally [*ex aequo*] favoreth all that be comprehended under the communion of one shape, form, and fashion," that is, she treats with the same impartiality all the members of the same species, who share the same nature in common. Nature bids and moves one to help all one's fellow men, as well as one's self, to a life full of joy and free from care. The logical conclusion from this truth is that "verily she commandeth thee to use diligent circumspection that thou do not so seek for thine own commodities that thou procure others' incommodities." This, therefore, is always the condition for good and true pleasure: "so that it may be gotten without wrong or injury" (*ad quod neque per iniuriam tenditur*). For it is "open wrong" (*iniuria*) to "let another man of his pleasure whiles thou procurest thine own."

This principle is the basis for the superb justice, both commutative and legal, of the Utopians. It is the basis, first of all, of commutative justice, by which a private person renders to another private person what is due to him by right. This kind of justice is exercised especially in contracts, whether gratuitous (such as promises or gifts) or onerous (such as purchases and sales, which, of course, can have no place, strictly speaking, among the communistic Utopians themselves, but only among their neighbors). Hence, the firm conviction of the Utopians is that "covenants and bargains made among private men ought to be well and faithfully fulfilled, observed, and kept." The same principle is the foundation for legal justice, by which citizens give to the community what is due to it in order to procure the common or social good. Legal justice is satisfied principally by the observance of good and just laws. These laws must be such as "other a good prince hath justly published or else the people, nother oppressed with tyranny nother deceived by fraud and guile, hath by their common consent constitute[d] and ratified." This insistence upon justice is aimed against the rich in European countries who make laws out of the "means and crafts" by which they endeavor to safeguard their ill-gotten gains and further oppress the poor with impunity. The laws which in particular must be observed carefully and scrupulously are those which deal with "the partition of the commodities of life, that is to say, the matter of pleasure." Here Hythloday certainly has his eye upon the neglect and nonexecution of the acts to remedy the evils arising from the enclosure of the commons. From as early as the fourth year of the reign of Henry VII, 1488–89, to as late as the seventh year of the reign of Henry VIII, 1515, Parliament passed acts against the pulling down of country towns and houses. Hythloday seems to be echoing the very words of these acts when he insists: "make a law that they which plucked down farms and towns of husbandry shall build them up again." This law should have been carried out, since it dealt with the vital problem of "the partition of the commodities of life." Failure to observe the statute resulted in ever-increasing poverty and unemployment, thievery and robbery.

Provided that just laws on the proper distribution of wealth and property are observed and are left inviolate, the Utopians consider it prudent sagacity to take care of one's own interests, and filial devotion to look to the public interests as well. But the deprivation of pleasure from one's fellow men as the price of securing one's own is patent injustice. On the contrary, to deprive one's self of something in order to give it to another is the friendly service of humanity and kindness. This latter is always a greater gain than loss. The gain, in fact, is three-fold: (1) compensation in the form of a return of favors, (2) greater pleasure (the consciousness of a deed well done and the remembrance of the love and good will of those benefited) coming to the soul than would have come to the body if one had not deprived oneself, and (3) the reward by God of "a short and small pleasure with great and everlasting joy." Epicurus himself, Plutarch tells his reader, says that "it is not only more beautiful to confer than to receive a benefit, but also more pleasurable, for nothing produces gladness as much as benefi-cence."

Such, then, are the four qualifications which the Utopians require for pleasure, true and worthy of the name. The practical result is that the standards of morality set for these devotees of pleasure turn out to be as stringent and high as those established by the Stoic, or even Christian, defenders of virtue.

The Utopians have fixed with great exactness the nature and the attributes of true pleasure. They have not, however, done the same in regard to false pleasures. Four causes, however, are mentioned in the course of the treatment of false pleasure: bodily illness, base desires, false opinions, and, above all, perverted habits. (1) Sickness or disease, to be understood in its physical rather than moral sense, is once as-signed as a cause of a corrupted judgment in regard to pleasure, but there seems to be no further discussion or mention of this cause. Thus, a sick or diseased man may like some things abhorred by a healthy person. (2) "The perverse and malicious flickering enticements of lewd and unhonest desires" (*peruersa improbarum cupiditatum il-lecebra*) cause many things which are unpleasant of themselves to be considered "not only for special and sovereign pleasures, but also be counted among the chief causes of life." These unrighteous desires have for their object, not only purely sensual pleasures as food and drink in immoderate quantities or of excessive delicacy, but also inordinate attachments to riches and honors. (3) Desires of a perverse and immoral nature, when yielded to without reserve, warp the mind with "a false opinion of pleasure." The result is that men who are deceived in this way choose from among false pleasures as if they surpassed other pleasures "by nature and not by their mistaking" (*natura non errore*). Intellectual error or wrong thinking, therefore, causes mortals to choose false pleasures. (4) Seduced into errors of judgment by alluring desires, men become victims of *corrupt habits or customs*. They look upon false pleasures as true pleasures since they do, as a matter of fact, derive gratification from them. Nevertheless, "not the nature of the thing but their perverse and lewd custom [*peruersa consuetudo*] is the cause hereof, which causeth them to accept bitter or sour things for sweet things, even as women with child, in their vitiate[d] and corrupt taste, think pitch and tallow sweeter than any honey." Driven by disease or incited by desire, they drive out nature with a "second nature," namely, habit, and judge false pleasures to be real pleasures. Whether the perverse habit or the erroneous judgment comes first is not clear. The quotation just given favors custom, since the next sentence speaks of a "man's judgment, depraved and corrupt . . . by custom." Nevertheless the judgment remains more important, since Hythloday is trying to explain why men set false values on deceitful and dishonest pleasures. The psychological sequence in most cases would be base desires impelling to perverse habits and perverse habits leading to erroneous judgments on the nature of pleasure.

Six to eight years later (*ca.* 1522), More was to apply a similar statement to sin. The pleasure of sin, too, is painful, but "we cannot perceive [it] for bitter, for the corruption of our custom whereby sour seemeth us sweet." Here, too, he assigns error and custom as the reason for our preference of bodily pleasure to spiritual delight, using the very example he had employed in *Utopia:*

> . . . like as a sick man feeleth no sweetness in sugar, and some women with child have such fond lust that they had liefer eat tar than treacle and rather pitch than marmalade, and some whole people love tallow better than butter, . . . so we gross carnal people, having our taste infected by the sickness of sin and filthy custom of fleshly lust, find so great liking in the foul and stinking delectation of fleshly delight that we list not once prove what manner of sweetness good and virtuous folk feel and perceive in spiritual pleasure.

He keeps insisting that it is "our blind custom" which makes us persevere in "the gross and filthy pleasure of all fleshly delight" and keeps us ignorant and "without care or cure" of "the sweetness of spiritual pleasure"—"as a sow content with draff, dirt, and mire careth neither for better meat nor better bed." Erasmus wrote truly in one of his adages that "no one is easily drawn away from vices in which he has been born and reared; for, things which in themselves are foul, seem beautiful and sweet because recommended by daily habit."

The false pleasures picked out by the Utopians for special condemnation are the following: (1) the erroneous notion that the better the clothes, the better men the wearers; (2) foolish pride in useless honors, especially in poverty-stricken nobility; (3) puerile delight in precious stones and gems, or in buried gold, or in riches kept merely for contemplation; and (4) mad enthusiasm for diceplay, hawking, and hunting. It is essential to note that, when Hythloday speaks of custom as the source of error in respect to pleasure, he is referring, not only to the corrupt habits of men as individuals, but also to the false estimates and vices of social classes, even of contemporary society as a whole. For a society furnishes the environment in which erroneous opinions can spring up and grow; in fact, a society can, and does, insinuate or foist its false notions on each generation as it rises. Thus, hunting can become a national false pleasure, as it did in the England of the period; and honors and riches, an international false pleasure, as in the Europe of the late Middle Ages and the Renaissance.

False pleasures are countless (*innumera*). Individuals, classes, nations, and even the ordinary run of mortals, may mistake innumerable opinions and activities for pleasures. The Utopians remain undaunted by such formidable opposition because they realize that *by nature* such pursuits have no sweetness in them and that, therefore, they "have no affinity with true and right pleasure." Their opponents answer that their amusements must be true pleasures for the reason that they do flood the senses with sweetness—a function which belongs to pleasure. The response of the Utopians is that the cause of the sweetness is not the *nature* of the thing, but, as has been seen, bodily illness, inordinate desires, errors of judgment, and, above all, evil custom or habit. For example, honey by its very nature is sweet and delectable. The lovers of false pleasure can supplant original nature with a second nature, namely, custom or habit; they can come to like pitch and tallow better than honey. But this subjective preference of individuals or groups cannot change the objective character of a true pleasure. Honey will always remain sweeter and more pleasant than pitch and tallow—because it is so by nature. The taste of pitch cannot become a true pleasure because it is "against nature" (*praeter naturam*). Mortals can change the name, but not the nature, of pleasure. The nature of pleasure, as good or as bad, is immutable.

# The Divided Mind

## by David M. Bevington

Students of *Utopia* are divided in their interpretation of Thomas More's political and economic opinions. Is More himself for or against common ownership of property? Writers on the question have tended to fall into two clearly defined camps, according to mankind's innate tendency to be born into this world as "either a little Liberal, Or else a little Conservative," and the polemical conflict between the factions has assumed in the context of our uneasy modern world the proportions of ideological warfare. The revered name of Thomas More has been invoked in support of the radical socialist states of the Soviet world empire, as well as in support of the anti-Communist position of the Papacy. Both interpretations purport to be founded on a critical reading of *Utopia*.

One literary reason why *Utopia* has lent itself to such divergence of opinion is its basic genre: the dialogue. More's island community is essentially the focal point for an extended discussion on government and society between various speakers or *personae*, each a character created by the author and having his individual point of view: Peter Giles, Hythloday, and the *persona* More who may or may not represent the views of Thomas More the writer. Giles's part in the discussion is minor, but Hythloday and *persona* More present two fundamental sides to the question. Hythloday's platform is the common ownership of property, and he refuses to concede the feasibility of gradual reform in a monarchical society. The *persona* More is often forthrightly opposed to the doctrine of common ownership, and argues instead for a policy of compromise and slow change within the limitations of practical politics. Their dialogue concludes in apparent lack of reconciliation of these opposing points of view. Accordingly, the critic can choose his hero. If Thomas More speaks directly for himself through the name of More, as he does in his later dialogues against Tyndale, then Hythloday is a dangerous public enemy like Tyndale whose

From *David M. Bevington, "The Dialogue in* Utopia: *Two Sides to the Question,"* Studies in Philology, *LVIII (1961), 496–509. Reprinted by permission of the University of North Carolina Press.*

dogmas are explicated only to be exploded.[1] If on the other hand Thomas More uses his own name merely as a protective device in order to propound through Hythloday an essentially subversive political philosophy, then the *persona* More may be viewed as a dupe or stooge, setting up straw men to be demolished in orderly succession by the invincible progressive.[2]

Between the cry of voices from both sides, the middle position of regarding *Utopia* as the impartial presentation of two points of view, as a dialogue of the mind with itself, has received less attention than it deserves.[3] The moderate stand is an unglamorous one. It does not have the ineluctable force of an idea carried to its logical absolute. Nevertheless the moderate position has much to commend itself in the writings of the eminently fairminded and humorously wise Thomas More. Our present purpose is to suggest the critical basis for supposing that Hythloday and *persona* More represent the two polarities of More's own mind, by an analysis of *Utopia* in terms of its genre and its historical perspective.

[1] W. E. Campbell, *More's Utopia and His Social Teaching* (London: Eyre & Spottiswoode, 1930). Campbell argues further that More himself considered *Utopia* to be a minor work, a *jeu d'esprit* describing an impossible dream world, which he wrote in Latin so as not to arouse the vulgar throng who might not understand. See also H. W. Donner, *Introduction to Utopia* (London: Sidgwick and Jackson, Ltd., 1945).

[2] The champion of the socialist interpretation, Karl Kautsky, is certain that the opinions of Thomas More are entirely in accord with those of Hythloday. In Kautsky's view *persona* More continually shifts his argument, concedes major points, and is finally worsted in every aspect. His objections to communal property-sharing are the conventional ones—lack of incentive and lack of authority—and only set the stage for Hythloday's demonstration of the manner in which such difficulties are solved in the communal state. The fact that the real Thomas More wished to apply the socialist remedy to his own society is evidenced by his role as member of and spokesman for the rising middle class, in revolt against aristocracy and feudalism. *Thomas More and His Utopia*, trans. H. J. Stenning (New York: International Publishers, 1927). See also Russell Ames, *Citizen Thomas More and His Utopia* (Princeton, N. J.: Princeton University Press, 1949).

[3] Only recently have critics become interested in following Sir James Mackintosh's suggestion, that More regarded various aspects of his *Utopia* "with almost every possible degree of approbation and shade of assent." Quoted in J. H. Lupton, ed., *The Utopia of Sir Thomas More* (Oxford, 1895), p. xli. Lupton too is of the opinion that criticism has often attempted "to crystallize what More purposely left in a state of solution" (p. xli). The moderate Catholic point of view has recently been presented with admirable clarity by Edward L. Surtz, S.J., *The Praise of Pleasure: Philosophy, Education, and Communism in More's Utopia* (Cambridge, Mass.: Harvard University Press, 1957), who declares that "More's personal attitude is manifested absolutely and unconditionally in neither [speaker More or Hythloday], but in both" (p. 182). See also Surtz, "Thomas More and Communism," *PMLA*, LXIV (1949), 549–64; R. J. Schoeck, "More, Plutarch, and King Agis: Spartan History and the Meaning of *Utopia*," PQ, XXXV (1956), 366–75; and Fritz Caspari, *Humanism and the Social Order in Tudor England* (Chicago: The University of Chicago Press, 1954), pp. 50–75.

As a literary technique, the dialogue is often used for purposes of refutation, for demonstrating the patent superiority of one idea over another. In this method the creator of the dialogue possesses the enviable advantage of being able to speak on behalf of his opponent, and to order his arguments in a fashion best suited to his own case. To such a type More's diatribes against Tyndale unquestionably belong.[4] Abstractly considered, however, literary dialogue would seem to lend itself equally well to a rendering of two balanced sides of a question. Such dialogue partakes of the nature of the drama: its author can create characters who speak as representatives of the many divisions of humanity. In analyzing a dramatic work we guard ourselves against identifying its author with any one of the characters, however much we may want to believe that some character summarizes our view of the author's mind. In this connection it is worth noting the kinds of early sixteenth-century drama with which More was most likely to be familiar: e.g., *Fulgens and Lucrece* (printed by John Rastell, More's brother-in-law), and a little later the interludes of John Heywood (More's nephew by marriage).[5] Nearly all of these interludes are characterized primarily by the element of rhetorical debate rather than dramatic action, and often present several sides of a question without preference for one side over the others. For example, Heywood's *Play of the Weather* reconciles all of Jove's petitioners with complete impartiality.

A balanced, two-sided dialogue is also analogous to the proceedings of a court trial, suggesting a parallel with the renowned impartiality of More's own judicial career. He served both as lawyer and judge on many occasions, and is known to have refused as a lawyer cases that he considered not worth a day in court. His overpowering sense of fairness inevitably found its way into his writings. Except for the occasions when he was refuting what he viewed as a palpable and gross public danger to society—such as a Tyndale or a Luther—More as a person was temperamentally inclined to grant any worthy cause a hearing and to arrive at the truth of the matter by the legal process of approaching every issue from two opposing viewpoints. As lawyer, More learned to argue for a case; as magistrate, he learned to receive conflicting arguments and to weigh them with justice.

[4] It is important to note that More's polemical dialogues tend to fall late in his career. The Reformation was to call forth in More the zealous defender of the Faith; in 1515–16 the atmosphere was one of less urgency, in politics as well as religion. When More wrote *Utopia* the time was not yet too late for dispassionate inquiry.

[5] A consideration of much non-dramatic debate in the fifteenth and early sixteenth centuries (e.g., Lydgate) leads to the impression that no firmly fixed line can be drawn between dramatic and non-dramatic debate. Some of Heywood's interludes, such as the *Play of Love,* are little more than forensic exercises presented between courses of a banquet.

More was capable, then, both of polemical dialogue and of a dialogue of genuine debate wherein real issues are to be decided. Which sort did he choose to employ in *Utopia*? An analysis of the literary method of this dialogue suggests that he viewed with detachment and fairness the presentation of both sides. The dialogue in Book I of *Utopia* contains a good deal more agreement than is generally supposed or recognized. Furthermore, the discussion moves in the direction of agreement. Amicable debate always is, or should be, a process of coming together, of discarding irrelevancies, of untangling those misunderstandings which are the artificial product of imperfect communication, of determining a basis of agreement in order to narrow the dispute to its elemental refinement of difference. The proponents concede points when convinced, until they have arrived at the distillation of their respective stands. Hythloday and *persona* More follow this generalized pattern, with the result that by the time they have discovered their ultimate positions they have left behind them a vast area of consent. They agree particularly with respect to their analysis of the historical facts: the condition of European society and government in the years of the early sixteenth century.

It is actually Peter Giles who begins the central discussion of Book I by posing the first major question, and accordingly it is important to account for More's literary purpose in introducing this third person to the conversation:

> Then Peter, much marvelling at the man: Surely, Master Raphael, quoth he, I wonder greatly why you get you not into some king's court.

Giles is indeed something of an innocent, for he supplements his query with two reasons for joining a king's court which are immediately demolished: (1) an official position in the government will enable a man to assist all his friends and kinsmen, and (2) public power will give a man an opportunity to bring himself "in a very good case," that is, to line his own pocket. These considerations are raised only to be answered, and Hythloday wastes little time or effort in doing so. Concerning favoritism and personal aggrandizement there could be no dispute, nor would it have been appropriate for either of the two main contenders to have proposed such possibilities. We may see here the usefulness of having a third person present at a dialogue essentially between two persons. Giles's function is to pose the question and to state the superficial arguments that would be unsuited to either of his companions. Thereafter his part in the discussion dwindles to nothing. Throughout the rest of Book I Hythloday continually addresses "Master More" with only one mention of Giles, and Peter's only speech in all this time is another touch of simpleheaded complacency: "Surely, quoth Master Peter, it shall be hard for you to make me believe that there is better order in that new land than is here in these countries that we know." [6]

It is doubtful that More wished deliberately to portray his good friend Giles as an intellectual lightweight. Clearly, More is consciously distinguishing between the *persona* and the actual man. Giles speaks in such conventional terms for dramatic reasons only. His function is an important one, for it is in the discrediting of Giles's suggestions of personal advantage and favoritism that Hythloday and *persona* More come to their first agreement. In fact, the very earliest utterance of *persona* More in the discussion is in support of Hythloday's deft answers to Giles:

> Well, I perceive plainly, friend Raphael, quoth I, that you be desirous neither of riches nor of power; and truly I have in no less reverence and estimation a man of your mind than any of them all that be so high in power and authority.

Whenever we find an agreement between the two principals, we are surely safe in assuming the author's concurrence. In the analogy of the courtroom, it is as though plaintiff and defendant have stipulated concerning some fact that is plainly incontrovertible. Thus, at the beginning of his trial on the merits and limitations of counselling a king, More rejects out of hand the consideration of private gain. In fact, the case is put far more strongly: Hythloday and *persona* More agree that court service, if it is to be undertaken, must prove a real personal sacrifice on the part of the philosopher. The greatest loss will be liberty, insists Hythloday: "Now I live at liberty after mine own mind and pleasure, which I think very few of these great states and peers of realms can say." And *persona* More readily concedes that public office will be "somewhat to your own pain and hindrance." The only point of contention between them is whether or not the result would be worth the self-sacrifice; that is, whether court service would prove to be a public benefit. Both speakers agree that personal comfort must never stand in the way of "the profit of the weal-public," but they differ as to whether the philosopher can be of use at all, no matter what the individual cost.

The chief question is: if the philosopher offers counsel, will the king take heed and will he translate good advice into wise policy? Which way does monarchy tend, to tyranny or to benevolence? Hythloday and *persona* More take sides from the start. For Hythloday, the record is almost entirely on the side of tyranny. To *persona* More, monarchy is at least a potential source of good, although he freely

---

[6] In answer to Kautsky, who contends that *persona* More is only posing the conventional arguments (see note 2, above), it might be argued that Peter Giles is the real dupe or stooge, not either of the chief contenders.

recognizes even at the beginning of the discussion the equal power for evil: "For from the prince, as from a perpetual well-spring, cometh among the people the flood of all that is good *or evil*" (italics mine). *Persona* More's position is not naive, like that of Giles. His statement is cautious but hopeful. Hythloday also speaks with qualifications about "the most part of all princes." In neither case is monarchy absolutely good or absolutely bad. Once again we find the spokesmen not so far apart as it first seemed. They agree that monarchy exists in various degrees of quality. The question hereupon becomes, for the philosopher who is to make the personal decision whether or not to offer counsel, what are the specific historical conditions at the time and place of his choice? In Thomas More's case, this meant England under the reign of Henry VIII.

Unquestionably an ambiguity existed in More's mind concerning the nature of the reigning monarch. Henry VIII was a young king of many virtues and liabilities. To More's sorrow Henry vaingloriously insisted on emulating his great ancestor Henry V in "delight in warlike matters and feats of chivalry" to the neglect of home administration and to the depletion of the treasury. Yet at his succession in 1509 Henry was immensely popular. He was amiable and generous, skillful in archery and tennis. He was competent in Latin, French, and Italian, was a musician and encourager of the arts, and a friend to new sciences and Humanism. Hence there was a contemporary validity in each of the respective stands of Hythloday and *persona* More.[7] More, the lawyer and judge, argues each case as one who understands the issues involved. His presentation takes the form of a comprehensive and orderly historical survey of recent issues and events, embracing three chief areas of governmental activity: (1) domestic policy: unemployment, the farm problem, the penal code and question of capital punishment, and vagabondage, (2) foreign policy, principally concerning foreign conquest and colonization, and (3) fiscal policy: the valuation of money, benevolences and forced loans, monopoly grants, extortion, and bribery.

In the technique of literary dialogue, the factor which distinguishes the discussion of domestic policy from the other two major headings is that it does not take place between Hythloday and *persona* More. Hythloday relates it to his companions as an argument that took place many years before, in 1497, among himself, Cardinal Morton, and "also a certain layman cunning in the laws of your realm." The possible reasons for this removal in time are several. One obvious suggestion is that it is a form of self-protection for the author, an attack on

[7] In an epigram entitled "The Good and the Bad Prince," More had defined the polarities thus: "What is a good prince? A sheepdog, who keeps away the wolves? And a bad prince? The wolf himself." Quoted in Kautsky, *Thomas More*, p. 125.

Henry VIII under the guise of criticizing a former reign. Another possibility is that the author is paying careful heed to his fictitious chronology, and accordingly dates Hythloday's visit to England at a time consonant with his voyages under the flag of Amerigo Vespucci. In the context of our discussion, however, a third reason may be offered: that the writer More's chief motivation is a removal of these specific issues from the immediacy of the Hythloday–*persona* More debate. Hythloday and *persona* More are enumerating the counts for and against English monarchy in 1515–16; we shall see, however, that domestic policy was not an issue wherein either of them found Henry VIII seriously at fault. Hence it was no longer a live issue in terms of the debate between More's two *personae*. We never actually learn *persona* More's opinion on the question of enclosure. At the conclusion of Hythloday's account he acknowledges that the narrator has spoken "wittily and so pleasantly," but implies that the entire matter of the speech has been slightly irrelevant to their debating point:

> But yet, all this notwithstanding, I can by no means change my mind, but that I must needs believe that you, if you be disposed and can find in your heart to follow some prince's court, shall with your good counsels greatly help and further the commonwealth.

In other words, *persona* More gently reproves his friend for beating a dead horse, and proposes that they proceed to matters that will really test the nature of Henry VIII's intentions. Why does he consider the discussion of enclosure to be irrelevant?

When we read Hythloday's stirring pleas on behalf of the husbandman, and his defiance of the rich, we instinctively conjecture a denunciation of complacent governmental policy, and suppose that Hythloday has scored a telling point against Henry VIII. In point of fact, however, by 1515–16 the government was attempting to handle the crisis on a large scale, under the direction of Wolsey.[8] Royal commissioners were appointed to study the problem, and they reported a need for positive action. Hythloday urges the government to "make a law"; important legislation was passed in 1514, 1515, and 1516. These acts were directed particularly against the evils which Hythloday mentions: engrossing and forestalling (i.e., buying up in advance to force up the market price), and the plucking down of farms and villages by rich men who were exploiting the demand for wool at the expense of other types of agriculture. The government actually ordered rebuilding, as Hythloday demands, and restrained numberless attempts at further enclosure. The problem continued, because it was too large an agricultural revolution to be stayed by any governmental policy;

[8] J. H. Hexter, *More's Utopia: The Biography of an Idea* (Princeton, N. J.: Princeton University Press, 1952), pp. 152–53.

but there was at least no ambiguity in the government's position on the farm problem. Hythloday's strictures would have been relevant in 1497, but not in 1516. Hence More removes this topic from the present conversation not only in time but in persons involved in the discussion.

The debate on domestic policy is a discussion within a discussion, and in many ways it mirrors in microcosm the larger plan. The most striking resemblance is that we again find three persons present at a dialogue (the scoffer and the friar appear from nowhere much later in the conversation). Once again the function of the third party—the irascible lawyer—is to serve as spokesman for the wrong point of view, and thus provide a basis of agreement between the principal characters. *Persona* Morton, like *persona* More, tends somewhat to the cautious side, but he receives Hythloday's declamation on enclosure reform without an objection. He is also willing to give the Polylerites' penal code a practical trial by deferring death sentences in England for a period of time, and adds his own suggestion that "vagabonds may very well be ordered after the same fashion." This amicable talk ends in a quarrel between the scoffer and the friar which has all the appearances of a digression. Hythloday afterwards apologizes to his hearers for a "long and tedious . . . tale." A digression it may be, but it is not without purpose. The sharp tongues and short tempers of lawyer, scoffer, and friar provide a meaningful contrast to the sane and considerate conduct of Hythloday, Morton, and *persona* More. The primary object of the satire in this digression is not the court or the clergy, but the folly of unreasonable argument.

The proposals concerning social legislation and penal reform are included in the Morton–Hythloday conversation for a very different reason from that suggested for the inclusion of the enclosure problem in this same section. In this latter instance the reason was that governmental policy seemed to be entirely in accord with More's wishes. The same could hardly be said to hold true for relaxation of the death penalty or improvement of regulations concerning vagabondage. Paradoxically, the precise opposite was true. In exploring these possibilities More was centuries ahead of his time, and his suggestions clearly extended beyond what he was ready to ask realistically of Henry VIII. No sixteenth-century government considered such social benevolence as its proper sphere of activity, much less as its duty. Hence it was an unfair test in distinguishing between a tyrant and a true prince at that point in history. More evidently had no doubt as to the essential rightness of this stand—both Hythloday and Morton agree to this—but More was not ready to propound such an advanced degree of enlightenment as a necessary condition of the philosopher's endorsement of any particular administration. In order to distinguish between the attainable and the unattainable, he relegated the latter to an abstracted conversation in a past reign. In summary, then, the material for the debate on domestic policy consists of a settled issue—enclosure—and an essentially impractical issue—social humanitarianism, both lying outside the realm of the central controversy concerning the nature of Tudor monarchy. It is for these disparate reasons that *persona* More can conclude the entire section with the easy dismissal, "But yet, all this notwithstanding, I can by no means change my mind." The crucial issues in the debate of the mind with itself lay yet ahead.

Plainly, it was to be in foreign and fiscal policy that monarchy would reveal its true inclination towards benevolence or despotism. The weight of evidence here would be decisive in persuading the philosopher to aid a government or to avoid its hopeless contamination. Policies of war and reckless expenditure were unavoidably interrelated, and were anathema to the Humanist scholar and supporter of London commercial interests.[9] If, however, one could reason that a young king's saber-rattling had stemmed from the effusion of adolescent vanity, one might pray for a change of temperament and for an era of peace at home. *Persona* More and Hythloday characteristically take sides. In the former's view any possibility for improvement, no matter how slight, would oblige the philosopher to assist and encourage the humane instinct. Hythloday is more inclined to expect the worst, and hints darkly at the incorrigible example of King Dionysius—with its obvious moral for the philosopher whose fate it is to be involved in duplicity beyond his control. Here is an issue that would influence one's choice, unlike the uncontroversial issue of domestic policy.

Consequently, in his consideration of foreign and fiscal policy the author shifts his scene from 1497 to the present (1516) and from the abstraction of a discussion within a discussion to the immediacy of the Hythloday–*persona* More debate. The foreign policy debate centers upon the example of the King of France, while fiscal policy is discussed abstractly with relation to "some king and his council." In neither case, obviously, is Henry VIII actually mentioned, and the extent to which his own actions partook of those evil examples is left unstated. The historical factors lie outside the scope of this study; we are interested in the literary method of debate and the extent of agreement between the two speakers.

In these terms, the fact of prime significance is that *persona* More and Hythloday agree entirely on the dangers involved. Although they implicitly differ as to whether Henry VIII in 1516 fell irretrievably into these categories of aggressive foreign policy and reckless spending,

---

[9] A well-known example of More's opposition to Tudor fiscal policy was his successful defense against Henry VII's budgetary request for three fifteenths, forcing More's retirement from politics until the death of that king.

the two speakers do not question the essential perniciousness of these categories. In foreign policy the French king is plainly charged with meddling in affairs that are none of his business: laying claim to foreign dominions under pretext of an ancient hereditary line of succession, buying soldiers and alliances, encouraging pretenders to the enemy's throne, and the like. *Persona* More makes no pretence of finding a glimmer of hope in such a situation. When asked how well he thinks the French king would receive the philosopher's advice to "tarry still at home" and govern his own kingdom wisely, *persona* More readily concedes the point: "So God help me, not very thankfully, quoth I." In a case like this, any philosopher would show his greatest wisdom in sparing his breath and saving his own skin.

Similarly in fiscal policy *persona* More has no answer for Hythloday's example of "some king and his council" who indulge in extortion, bribery, "benevolences" and forced loans, creating exorbitant taxes (largely at the expense of the middle class) for the purpose of levying unneeded troops. After stating his proposals and objections, Hythloday concludes:

> These, and such other information, if I should use among men wholly inclined and given to the contrary part, how deaf hearers think you should I have?
> Deaf hearers doubtless, quoth I, and in good faith no marvel.

When confronted with completely "deaf hearers," *persona* More is ready to abandon the cause of counselling a monarch, and to live in philosophic retirement with Hythloday, pondering an impractical but ideal world across the oceans. But who is to say that an administration at any particular moment in history is entirely hopeless? Hythloday's examples of evil are as theoretical in their way as his picture of the ideal life of Utopia in Book II.

Somewhere between the ideally good and the perfectly evil stood Henry VIII, and his intentions were as yet uncertain. Thomas More had to make a decisive choice in answer to Henry's request for his wise counsel. The actual decision is beyond our present scope, but it is central to an understanding of the dialogue to realize that in 1515–16 More perceived a dilemma.[10] He gave expression to it in a pattern of

[10] J. H. Hexter presents a convincing thesis that it was a continuation of peace— as a part of Wolsey's policy of retrenchment and non-intervention until the balance of power should realign itself with the death of the old men Frederick of Spain and Maximilian of the Holy Roman Empire—which provided a conclusive impetus for More's final decision to join the government in 1518. *More's Utopia*, pp. 132–57. Compare Caspari, *Humanism*, who believes with Russell Ames that More "probably entered royal service in 1516 after much hesitation" [Fritz Gaspari, *Humanism and the Social Order in Tudor England* (Chicago: University of Chicago Press, 1954), p. 226, n. 10].

two alternatives: Hythloday's wariness of all Machiavellianism as an earnest of future ill intent, and *persona* More's cautiously idealistic tendency to seize upon any ray of hope as a basis for gradual improvement.

Now that the historical evidence is in, More's spokesmen proceed to their summations, to the concluding arguments of counsel for both sides. If one spokesman is merely serving as devil's advocate for the other, it is difficult to understand why both addresses to the jury are so coherent, rational, convincing, and essentially moderate in tone. *Persona* More labels the distinction between their points of view with the terms "school philosophy" (Hythloday's) and "another philosophy, more civil" (his own). He does not use the term "school philosophy" pejoratively; it is "not unpleasant among friends in familiar communication." [11] Its only fault is that it is too forthright, too uncompromising; it lacks the quality of tact and diplomacy, of knowing when to speak and when to remain silent. "Civil" philosophy is the ability to "make the best of it," to "handle the matter wittily and handsomely for the purpose; and that which you cannot turn to good, so to order it that it be not very bad." This is no idle and naive humor, to be overturned and made ridiculous by Hythloday. More as a responsible public servant had long known the meaning of "compromise" in its best sense. He was eminently a practical man of politics.

Yet a man of principle knows where compromise leaves off and appeasement begins. At least, he knows in theory. More's beloved classical master Seneca found the dividing line to be exasperatingly thin and hard to locate. A policy of compromise involves a frightening element of chance. In a very real sense, compromise is a braver course for the true man of principle than stoical indifference. The counsellor of state is forever in need of reappraising the situation, while the man of principle stands fast on his logic. The worst that can befall the latter is martyrdom. The counsellor is in danger of personal dishonor and ridicule. Nero's reign might well have been the worse without Seneca's attempts at compromise, but the stigma of "appeaser" will live forever with Seneca's name. More evidently had Seneca's example in mind as he wrote *Utopia,* for he refers to the passage "out of *Octavia* the place wherein Seneca disputeth with Nero."

It is possible to be at the same time a counsellor of state and a man of principle—possible but dangerous. At every moment in history such a man must decide whether to acquiesce or to stand fast. He holds as incontrovertible the axiom that "You must not forsake the ship in a tempest because you cannot rule and keep down the winds." On the

[11] Caspari, *Humanism,* identifies Hythloday's point of view with that of Erasmus, supposing conversations between Erasmus and More much like those in Book I of *Utopia* (p. 52).

other hand, no sane man would undertake to contravene Plato's similitude of the philosophers who, being unable to persuade others to come in out of the rain, "do keep themselves within their houses, being content that they be safe themselves, seeing they cannot remedy the folly of the people." More, in his own life, applied both courses of action to differing problems. The problem relevant to the dialogue in *Utopia* was a complex one, and depended on a great many variables. The choice was not easy, and by all indications it came months or even years after the composition of the work. What we hear in *Utopia* is the dispassionate voice of the author, laying before the world his view of the facts and of the philosophical basis for a decision.

The description of the island of Utopia in Book II deals similarly with the problem of the philosopher in deciding whether or not to participate in a government. The respective stands of *persona* More and of Hythloday are merely the obverse of their previous positions concerning tyranny. The former, who always tries to "make the best of it," is skeptical of a system that would overthrow entirely the established order of things. He is skeptical but not hostile; he is anxious to hear his friend's account of Utopia in all its details: "you shall think us desirous to know whatsoever we know not yet." Hythloday, who considers most princes to be beyond hope, is ready to try a more severe remedy. Yet even he does not reject the moderate solution out of hand. He readily grants that wise statutes may help somewhat to ease inequality of wealth, so that "these evils also might be lightened and mitigated. But that they may be perfectly cured, and brought to a good and upright state, it is not to be hoped for, whiles every man is master of his own to himself." The description of Utopia is a body of theoretical material towards which More's inquiring mind develops a polarity of rational attitudes. The philosophical mind must contain within itself always a Platonic ideal as a frame of reference. Nothwithstanding, the Platonist in his worldly life is a practical man, recognizing the need for temporizing with human imperfection. *Persona* More is this practical man. It is he who accentuates mortal frailty: "For it is not possible for all things to be well unless all men were good, which I think will not be yet this good many years." Still, Utopia belongs to the future; and *persona* More's practicality remained a living force for its author in his life's application of Utopian ideals to English society. The two sides of the question continued for More to be valid and essentially unanswerable.

# A Detestable State

## by T. S. Dorsch

That great More scholar R. W. Chambers claims that *Utopia* "looks back to the *Republic* and *Laws* of Plato, and initiates a long series of 'Ideal Commonwealths.'" More was acquainted with these works of Plato when he wrote his *Utopia,* but I can find in its spirit and purpose no close debt to them, not even in the references to the *Republic* at the end of Book I, which are not developed there and are not carried over into Book II; nor are there any significant resemblances other than that all three works represent commonwealths which exist only in the minds of their creators, and almost of necessity cover a certain amount of common ground. Surely C. S. Lewis is much closer to the mark. . . . Following his method in arranging the books on my shelves, I should place *Utopia* next to my copy of the works of Lucian, for I see it primarily as a Lucianic "true history" appended to a partly Lucianic dialogue. I believe that the clue to the understanding of Book II may be found in the words with which Lucian closes the preface to his *True History*: "I am writing about things entirely outside my own experience and anyone else's, things that have no reality whatever and never could have. So mind you do not believe a word I say." I suggest that Erasmus, himself an appreciative reader of Lucian, as is shown no less by his *Praise of Folly* than by his translation of one of the dialogues—that Erasmus and More's other contemporaries found *Utopia* an amusing or "iollye" book precisely because they did not believe a word that More said in his description of the Island of Utopia; they gave themselves up to its spirit of fantasy and comedy, and took from between the lines whatever there was in it that was intended to be taken seriously. They read it as they read Lucian.

\* \* \*

At this point we must recall that *Utopia* is in two books, which cannot be treated alike. In Book I More is not writing about things that

*From T. S. Dorsch, "Sir Thomas More and Lucian: An Interpretation of* Utopia," Archiv für das studium der neueren sprachen und literaturen, *CCIII (1967), excerpted from 349–63. Reprinted by permission of the author.*

are outside his own experience and that have no reality whatever; he is writing about the England and the Europe of his own day; he is describing evils and abuses that actually existed, and considering how they may be remedied. It is only in Book II that he writes about a place that never did and never could exist—a no-place. The Lucianic dialogue form is appropriate to the one set of circumstances, the Lucianic "true history" to the other.

More opens Book I by establishing his setting for the dialogue and introducing his characters. In company with Cuthbert Tunstall, at that time Master of the Rolls, he has been sent to Flanders, he tells us, as an ambassador of Henry VIII. At Antwerp he has formed a close friendship with Peter Giles, secretary to the municipality of that city, and it is Giles who introduces him to an impressive bearded stranger, Raphael Hythloday by name, who becomes the main speaker in the ensuing dialogue in this book, and the narrator of the second book. He is learned, and as wise as Ulysses, and he has travelled extensively; he accompanied Amerigo Vespucci in the last three of his famous voyages, and at other times travelled to many lands all over the world. He must obviously be listened to with great respect when he talks about any country he has visited. All this is rather like the opening of a historical novel. We are taken to a known locality at a particular moment in history, and meet a number of well-known historical persons. Once the accurate historical setting has been established, we are perfectly ready to accept the fictitious personages (like Hythloday) and fictitious events that are introduced into it. The opening pages of *Utopia* have all the verisimilitude of the best historical novels. It is a verisimilitude that has much in common also with that of Lucian and Swift when they describe in so much detail the beginnings of the voyages that involved their mariner-heroes in so many mischances in so many strange lands. The verisimilitude is increased when we learn that Raphael has spent some time in England, and that his pungent criticisms of Tudor England are brought forward in conversation with Cardinal Morton, in whose household More was brought up as a boy. We note in passing that, by precise historical references, More has prudently back-dated the period to which these criticisms refer to a time twelve years before Henry VIII came to the throne.

In the dialogue proper of Book I there are a number of "Lucianic" elements: the comic anecdotes, for example, such as those in which the friar and the jester figure; the ironical account of the land of the Polylerites; the proper names which are so evidently puns or jokes; the trivial objections which are so crushingly answered; the tone of the last section, in which the pros and cons of Utopianism are discussed. In the main, however, More concerns himself, or rather causes Raphael to show his concern, with the social evils of England—the swarms of beggars and thieves, the inhumanity of the legal system, the poverty and misery engendered by the inordinate growth of sheep-farming and the enclosure of land, the rapacity of landowners and merchants, the ambition and warlike propensities of European monarchs, the debasement of the coinage, and the unjust taxes and imposts. That the condition of the people of England was no better under Henry VIII than in the previous reign, and indeed became worse in Henry's later years, is attested by numerous writings of the period. The *Four Supplications* published by the Early English Text Society and the observations of such writers as Thomas Starkey and Henry Brinkelow all give the same grim picture of suffering and squalor.

Book I of *Utopia* is not here my special concern, but it has been necessary to touch on it because of its importance as a framework for Book II, and because it shows up by contrast something of what More aimed at doing in that book. In Book I he is dealing in hard, cruel truth; in spite of the irony and the humor, he is writing a *factual* social treatise.

When we turn to Book II, we are from the outset faced by some obvious joking; all the proper names, not just two or three as in Book I, are jokes. The name *Utopia,* as everyone knows, is derived from Greek words which give it the meaning of "not-place," or "no-place," with a possible pun also on "well-place," or "good-place." The fair and spacious capital city Amaurote is, by derivation from the Greek ἀμαυρός, a dim place which baffles the sight. Also deriving from the Greek, the name of the River Anyder means "waterless"; the Nephelogetes and the Alaopolitanes are cloud-dwellers and dwellers in a city of the blind; the Anemolians are a windy, insubstantial folk; and similarly all the other names embody jokes. Even the wise and learned Hythloday is a dealer-out of idle talk and nonsense, for that is what his name ὑθλοδαῖος signifies. We may ask ourselves how seriously we are to take this "exquisite platforme, paterne and example of a singuler good common wealth" when we are directed in this way to take it light-heartedly.

In the physical sense Utopia seems to be a very desirable place to live in. It is a beautiful and fertile island, well supplied by nature and by the foresight of King Utopus with good harbors and good defences. It abounds in all things necessary to life. Its fifty-four cities, all identically laid out, are "large and faire." The capital city Amaurote has a well-guarded supply of water; its streets are "set furth very commodious and handsome," and its houses are "buylded after a gorgious and gallante sorte" and backed by large gardens. There are four excellent hospitals, and an efficient health-service run by the state. In the countryside the farms are well-built, well-equipped, and well-organized. This account of the land and its cities must of course be accepted at

its face value. In elaborating it More deals many back-handed blows
at the very different conditions in his own England. However, the
writer who is cutting the pattern for a perfect commonwealth must
obviously begin by providing first-rate living conditions. These things
must be taken for granted in any utopia, as must the honest, hard-
working, healthy, intelligent citizens whom Raphael describes; the
citizens must be worthy of the beneficent system under which they live.
Things were not always like that, we are told, but through the generations the enlightened Utopians have brought the land and its amenities
to as nearly perfect a condition as could be envisaged in a human
community.

How are we to read the remainder of Book II, that is, everything
relating to the life and the customs of Utopia? We may begin by accept-
ing as a joke a small point at the beginning of the book, which has
nevertheless been cited as an example of More's advanced ideas. The
Utopians do not allow their hens to sit on their eggs, but "by keepynge
theym in a certayne equall heate they brynge lyfe into them, and hatche
theym. The chykens, as sone as they come oute of the shel, follow
men and women in steade of the hennes." It is a joke, of course, but it
is perhaps not without significance that the first practice of the Utopians that is described should be described in terms of a Lucianic *reductio ad absurdum,* and that it should be an unnatural practice.
However, More goes on to more serious matters.

"Warre or battel as a thing very beastly" the Utopians "do detest
and abhorre," although all their men every day, and all their women
on certain appointed days, have to spend some time in military training, in case they should be invaded, or called upon to fight on behalf
of their allies or of oppressed peoples. It is scarcely necessary to say
that More also hated war. The whole of his public life shows how
constantly he worked in the cause of peace—between private persons
as well as between nations; and he once told his son-in-law William
Roper that he would gladly let himself be tied up in a sack and cast
into the Thames, "upon condition three things were well established
in Christendome. . . . The first is, that where as the most part of
Christian princes be at mortall warrs, they weare at universal peace."
In Book I of *Utopia* he causes Raphael to manifest a similar hatred of
war, both in his picture of its grievous consequences and in his concern that "the moste parte of all princes have more delyte in warlike
matters . . . than in the good feates of peace." These princes "em-
ploye muche more study, how by right or by wrong to enlarge their
dominions, than howe wel and peaceablie to rule and governe that
they have alredie."

Considering their detestation of war, we may well be surprised to
see how often the Utopians find occasion to fight. They too study to

enlarge their dominions, and when they do so they drive out of the
territories "which they have limited and apointed for themselves" any
of the inhabitants who will not collaborate with them, "and if they
resiste and rebel, then they make warre agaynst them"; they justify this
on the grounds that they will make more profitable use of the land
than those whom they are replacing. No doubt the princes of Europe
used the same argument. Then the Utopians send armies to help allies
who are at war, not always, however, to help them to defend themselves, "but sometymes also to requite and revenge injuries before to
them done"—scarcely a reason for fighting that would commend itself
to an enlightened and humane people. They fought a "cruel and
mortall warre" for the Nephelogetes against the Alaopolitanes, and
reduced the great Alaopolitane nation to bondage, for no other cause
"but that the Nephelogete marchaunt men, as the Utopians thought,
suffred wrong of the Alaopolitanes." If a Utopian visitor chances to be
maimed or killed in another country, "onlesse the offenders be rendered unto them in recompence of the injurie, they will not be ap-
peased; but incontinente they proclaime warre against them." Raphael
narrates all this in a perfectly matter-of-fact way, but clearly implies
his approval. We must of course read his approval in reverse; More is
showing by the example of the Utopians some of the bad causes for
which wars are fought, and against which European princes should
guard themselves.

With some of the Utopian methods of warfare we are perhaps more
familiar today than were More's contemporaries. Their most valuable
weapon is the fifth column. They despise gold, but they collect great
stores of it, and what they do not require for the manufacture of
chamber-pots and fetters for their slaves ("useful utensils," as the Yale
editors euphemistically call them) they use for the spreading of dis-
affection in enemy territory. They promise rich rewards to anyone who
will kill their enemies' prince and leaders, and spend lavishly to make
traitors of as many enemy citizens as possible. "This custome of byinge
and sellynge adversaryes among other people is dysallowed, as a cruel
acte of a basse and a cowardyshe mynde," says Raphael; but the upright and enlightened Utopians "rejoyse and avaunt themselves, if they
vanquishe and oppresse their enemies by craft, and deceite." If fighting
cannot be avoided, they hire mercenaries from a nation renowned for
its savage and remorseless ways, ensuring their loyalty by offering them
higher wages than other nations can afford to pay; then they place
them in all the most dangerous posts, "from whens the mooste parte
of them never cummeth againe to aske their rewardes." After them they
use the soldiers of the country for which they profess to be fighting,
and then those of other allies; "when there is no remedy, but that they
muste needes fight themselves," they do so courageously, women as

well as men, all adult members of a family fighting side by side, for since it is a great dishonor for the husband to come home without his wife, the wife without her husband, the children without their parents, they will all fight to the death if one of them is killed. These are the main articles in the Utopian code of war, and Raphael appears to accept them as perfectly reasonable. We have already in Book I heard More's views on the employment of "hiered souldiours"; we can guess what he would have thought of the morality of the code as a whole. But indeed, there is no need for us to guess; everything relating to the Utopians' attitude to war and methods of conducting a war is described with an irony that could scarcely be missed.

For the last three of the years between 1527 and 1532, when Henry VIII was through every legal and ecclesiastical channel seeking sanction for his divorce from Catherine of Aragon, More was Lord Chancellor of England, the most important lay consultant in the matter of the divorce—he had indeed been consulted from the first. He spent anxious months pondering within himself, corresponding with theologians, and searching the Scriptures and the early Fathers. His conscience would not allow him to approve the divorce, and his opposition may be clearly seen as the first link in the chain that led to his execution for conscience' sake in 1535. Nor could he accept the validity of Henry's subsequent marriage to Anne Boleyn. *Utopia* was written a dozen years before the question of the divorce arose, but such is the consistency of More's life and beliefs that we cannot doubt that he would have arrived at the same decisions if they had been required of him at that time. "Whom God hath joined together let no man put asunder," says More's chief authority for his beliefs about marriage.

In Utopia, we are told, "matrymoneie is there never broken, but by death." In the same breath Raphael goes on, "except adulterye breake the bonde, or els the intollerable wayewarde maners of either partye." A few sentences later we learn that if a married pair "cannot well agree betwene themselfes," and find other persons "with whome they hope to lyve more quietlye and merylye," they may "by the full consente of them bothe be divorsed asonder and maried againe to other." Divorce is not, indeed, encouraged, and persistent adultery is punished by bondage, and even by death; but no great difficulties face those who seem to have reasonable pretexts for divorce. It is often argued that the liberal-minded More, as usual thinking in advance of his age, is facing the facts of life in permitting divorce and the remarriage of divorced persons in his enlightened commonwealth; the Yale editors, for example, state that his enactments on marriage and divorce spring "from consideration of the individual's happiness." He would of course have been shocked at the thought that the Utopian divorce laws should be allowed to operate in any real country. Again by the example of the Utopians, he is forcing his European readers to reflect upon the inviolability of the marriage-bond. Again, in fact, we must read him in reverse, as we read Lucian—and Swift.

Utopia has an excellent state health service, and the incurably sick are very well cared for. "But yf the disease be not onelye uncurable, but also full of contynuall payne and anguishe; then the priestes and the magistrates exhort the man . . . that he wyl determine with himselfe no longer to cheryshe that pestilent and peineful disease." They urge him either to take his own life or to let someone else put him out of his pain. They "cause none suche to dye agaynste his wyll," but none the less they "exhort" him to end his life. There are today many people who can reconcile the advocacy of euthanasia with their religious beliefs; More would have regarded them as vile heretics. To accept at its surface value Raphael's grave-faced approval of this Utopian practice is surely grossly to misread More's intention.

Nor can we take the section on Utopian education very seriously. The more closely it is read, the more obvious it becomes that it is introduced largely to provide opportunities for ironical observations on the super-subtle learning of European logicians and astrologers.

In Utopia "there be divers kindes of religion." Some worship the sun, the moon, or a planet. Some worship as the chiefest and highest god a man that was once of excellent virtue or of famous glory. Many "believe that there is a certayne godlie powre unknowen, everlastinge, incomprehensible, inexplicable, farre above the capacitie and retche of mans witte, dispersed throughoute all the worlde, not in bignes, but in vertue and power. Him they call the father of al." Raphael and his companions converted a number of Utopians to Christianity. Provided that he did not cast doubt on the immortality of the soul or the existence of a divine providence, or try to turn anyone to his own beliefs by overmuch persuasion or by violence, every Utopian had "free libertie and choise to believe what he woulde," for so the great King Utopus had in his wisdom ordained.

Now More was a stern opponent of freedom of religious belief. His longest works are works of religious controversy in which he pours mockery, scorn, and abuse, sometimes scurrilous abuse, upon Tyndale, Luther, and anyone else who has dared to question in the smallest point the doctrines or the authority of the Catholic Church. He regarded heresy as the most damnable of crimes because it brought damnation to human souls, and he protested against any relaxation of the laws by which heretics were tried and, if found guilty, condemned to be burnt. In all the other concerns of life he was the most kindly, humane, and tolerant of men; and indeed he would do everything in his power to bring heretics back into the fold. R. W. Chambers and other writers have brought forward convincing evidence to

show how often, and with what kindliness and patience, he tried to
dissuade heretics from their false beliefs; and he himself says in Chapter 49 of *The Apologye of Syr Thomas More:* "As touchynge heretykes,
I hate that vyce of theyrs and not theyr persones and very fayne wolde
I that the tone were destroyed, and the tother saved." On the other
hand, if the heretic will not put "that malycyouse folye oute of hys
poysened proude obstynate harte: I wolde rather be content that he
were gone in tyme, then over longe to tary to the destruccyon of
other." In Chapter 25 of the same work he expresses his approval of
the burning of certain heretics, whom he names; they were burnt
by the authorities of the Church, of course, for as a lay legal officer
he could have no say or hand in such punishments, except in so far
as it was his duty to hand over to the Church any man whom in his
own court he had adjudged guilty of heresy. But he strongly approved
of their punishment by burning. The long *Dialogue concerning Heresies,* written at the instance of the Bishop of London, is a vehement
attack on the Lutheran heresies and a closely-reasoned defense of all
the rites and ceremonies and doctrines of the Catholic Church; its
main theme is the infallibility of this Church and its absolute authority as the divinely guided interpreter of the Scriptures. The last five
books of the even longer *Confutation of Tyndale's Answer* are also
an elaborate argument that "The catholike knowen church cannot
erre." And a great part of the *Debellation of Salem and Bizance* is
devoted to a defense, often couched in the strongest terms, of the
laws against heretics. How often have we not read or been told that
*Utopia* is, among other things, a plea for religious toleration? But
has not More rather provided his own *reductio ad absurdum* of the
very thought of religious toleration (a notion unacceptable, surely, to
every Christian of his day) in allowing his Utopians to set up as the
chiefest and highest god the moon, a planet, a man?

Raphael's description of religion in *Utopia* cannot here be discussed in detail, but one further point must be touched on. The
priests, who may be either men or women, both officiating with equal
authority in all religious rites and ceremonies, are, like the magistrates,
chosen by secret ballot; and "the men priests . . . take to their wifes
the chiefest women in all their countreye." As his controversial writings
abundantly testify, there is nothing here that More would not have
condemned as wicked heresy, above all the marriage of the priests.
He regarded Luther's marriage as an act of wanton profligacy, all the
more reprehensible in that his wife had been a nun. Of many passages
that might be cited in evidence, one must suffice: in Book IV of the
*Dialogue* he asks why a hearing should be given to Luther, "to a fond
friar, to an apostate, to an open incestuous lecher, a plain limb of the
devil, and a manifest messenger of hell." On this particular "abhom-

inable heresye" of Luther's, as he describes it in the preface to the *Confutation*, he could scarcely make his position clearer. It seems reasonable to suggest that he placed Raphael's account of the religion of the Utopians at the end of his narrative as the grand climax to all that he most severely reprehended in their commonwealth.

Are we intended to approve of the philosophical beliefs of the Utopians, as Raphael seems to do? I doubt it. Not that these beliefs are in themselves harmful, or lacking in authority and respectability; but in the context of Book II as a whole, there is good reason, as I trust my analysis is showing, to be suspicious of anything that More allows Raphael to develop at all elaborately, as he develops the philosophical speculation of the Utopians. "They reason of vertue and pleasure," he says. More's readers would know that this reasoning of virtue and pleasure, described at some length as something that it is important to know about the Utopians, is taken straight from Aristotle and Cicero, with some added touches from the Stoic philosophy. Raphael is intent on showing his Utopians to be in every way an enlightened people. If More had wished us to regard the Utopians as truly enlightened thinkers, I cannot help feeling that he would, for all his admiration of the Greeks, have provided them, not with a ready-made pagan philosophy, but with something which, while it obviously could not be overtly Christian, came close to a Christian philosophy.

These are some of the larger issues covered in *Utopia*. The social organization of the Utopians may be dealt with more briefly. Everything is so efficiently organized that they all work the same hours, three before noon and three in the afternoon. Their cities, their farm communities, and the family groups in which they live are kept at uniform sizes, and if the numbers rise above those prescribed by the state, families or members of families are moved to make up deficiencies elsewhere or to colonize the dominions overseas. Indeed, they have no places that they can call their own, for every tenth year they must change their houses by lot. They have no holidays, apart from days of religious observance, for they may not make journeys or visits to friends in other neighborhoods without a licence from a magistrate, and if they are away from home for more than a day they cannot escape the obligation to do either a morning's or an afternoon's work every day. "Now you se," says Raphael, "how litle liberte they have to loiter: howe they can have no cloke or pretence to ydlenes."

At set hours the Utopians are summoned by trumpets to their meals in the communal halls, where the slaves—there are plenty of slaves—do the hard work and the women do the cooking. The men sit on one side of the tables, the women on the other. Boys and girls below the age of marriage wait on them, or else "stand by with marvailous silence" listening to the edifying conversation of the grown-ups; for their food they have to rely on what their elders give them from the tables, and sometimes they are forgotten and go hungry. The younger children are fed by their nurses in separate rooms. It is not forbidden to have an occasional meal in private, if there is any food to spare after the halls have been served, but the practice is frowned on. All spare-time recreations—if there is any true spare time—are designed to be profitable either to the mind or to the morals. There are no wine-taverns, no ale-houses, no "lurkinge corners"; all their diversions are provided for them in appointed places, so that "they be in the presente sighte, and under the eies of every man." They all dress exactly alike in woollen garments of "the natural coloure of the wul," one uniform for the men, one for the women, differing only between the married and the unmarried. They are brought up to despise any form of personal adornment, and gold and jewels are put to base uses.

The Utopians have no personal possessions; even in the houses there is nothing "that is private, or anie man's owne." The state owns and controls everything. There is no need for money; food, clothing, and all the other necessities of life are drawn from the state stores, and there are no luxuries, unless they can regard as a luxury the music that is played to them in the halls every evening during supper. There is no freedom of speech. One must guard one's tongue even when speaking of religion; and anyone who discusses politics anywhere but in the council-chamber, that is to say, anyone who talks politics other than in his official capacity as an officer of the state, is put to death. There are indeed many offences for which the penalty is either bondage or death. Everywhere Big Brother is on the watch.

This is not, I think, a biased account of life in Utopia. It is merely an account in which the facts of Raphael's narrative have been separated from the fantasy and comedy by which they are accompanied. R. W. Chambers argues that in *Utopia* More was describing a commonwealth that was as good as any commonwealth could be that was not founded on Christianity; the Utopians ordered their lives according to a "natural" religion and a "natural" system of morality. If the Utopians, unenlightened by Christianity, could do so well, what should not be expected of the Christian states of Europe? I cannot accept this interpretation, nor those of H. W. Donner, Paul Turner, the Yale editors (who claim that More's democracy is "an assembly of saints"), or anyone else who argues that More intended his Utopia to be regarded as a desirable, if scarcely attainable, ideal. These interpretations in no way accord with what we learn of him from his other writings and his letters, and from the unimpeachable testimony of Erasmus, Roper, and many other of his friends and contemporaries.

It seems scarcely necessary to demonstrate, item by item, what More would have found absurd or vicious in the life of the Utopians as

Raphael describes it. However, a few points may be taken up. As C. S.
Lewis has pointed out, in the *Confutation* More condemns communism as one of the "horrible heresies" of the Anabaptists, and in the
*Dialogue of Comfort* he defends private riches. He saw to it that all his
children married into families of wealth and standing. Although—
unknown to almost everyone but his daughter Margaret—he always
wore a hair-shirt, even during his long imprisonment, the Holbein
portraits show him wearing clothes appropriate to his high station,
and he had a costly gold chain round his neck when he was taken
to the Tower; in an epigram cited by Chambers he rejoices in the
pretty silken clothes that he gave to his daughters. For anyone but
heretics he deprecated severe punishments of the type so often meted
out by the Utopians; as a judge he was renowned no less for the
temperateness than for the justice of his judgments, and in another
epigram he reminds his daughters that, when he had found himself
compelled to punish them, he had beaten them with peacock feathers.
He would have abhorred the Utopian practice of dividing families,
and their various other forms of segregation. His own family—a large
one, for it included a number of relatives and dependants—was regarded by all who knew it as a model of unity, happiness, and mutual
love. All the time that he was travelling on the King's business he
longed to be at home, and he wrote endlessly to his children, and was
delighted by their letters to him in which they spoke of their everyday
concerns and their studies. He kept his own conscience inviolate over
the questions of the King's divorce and remarriage and the Act of
Supremacy, but at the same time insisted that all other men should
be allowed to speak and act according to the dictates of their con-
sciences.

To us today the drab uniformity and severe restrictiveness of the
life of the Utopians must seem repellent, the more so since we have
been made familiar with many of its features as they have been
manifested in modern totalitarian states. I hope I have shown that
it would seem no more repellent to us than it would have seemed to
More. And the way in which he makes his repulsion clear brings me
back to Lucian. I suggest that we shall not understand Book II of
*Utopia* unless we read it in the same way as we read Lucian—and
as we read *Gulliver's Travels*. We must accept as necessary properties
of any utopia the natural amenities of the island, the well-planned
cities, and the other things to which I referred earlier; in everything
that relates to the life and institutions of the Utopians we must read
Raphael's straight-faced approval in reverse. More's *Utopia* and Swift's
*Gulliver's Travels* are the two most beautifully developed and most
consistently sustained works of Lucianic irony in English literature.
Many readers have taken seriously the final paragraph of the book

in which More tells us that only considerations of hospitality and the reflection that Raphael must be tired after talking so long prevented him from taking up with him some questionable points in his narrative—he remembered, too, that Raphael did not take kindly to contradiction. The paragraph is, of course, instinct with More's characteristic irony, which reaches its climax in the final sentence: "As I cannot agree and consent to all thinges that he said . . . so must I nedes confesse and graunt that many thinges be in the Utopian weale publique, whiche in our cities I maye rather wishe for, then hope after."

This is not quite the last word. All great satirists write with a moral purpose. By showing us what we ought not to do and what we ought not to be, Lucian and Swift and More make us think about what we ought to do and what we ought to be. They are intensely serious and intensely moral writers. Their fantasy, their comedy, and their irony are their most effective means of exposing what is ridiculous or odious. As we have seen, Erasmus and More's other contemporaries enjoyed the fantasy and comedy of *Utopia;* it is impossible to believe that they did not at the same time appreciate its irony and understand its serious purport. C. S. Lewis called *Utopia* "a spontaneous overflow of intellectual high spirits . . . which starts many hares and kills none." Surely, like Lucian and Swift, More is in complete control of his flow of intellectual high spirits, and, again like Lucian and Swift, kills stone dead every hare that he starts.

## PART TWO

## View Points

## Sir Ernest Barker: *Utopia* and Plato's *Republic*

With the Renaissance came a new birth of [Plato's] *Republic*. The Platonism of the Florentine Academy and the circle which gathered round Lorenzo de Medici was indeed Neo-Platonic; but in the little farm at Montevecchio, Ficino had completed by 1477 his translation of Plato's writings into Latin. It is, however, in the *Utopia* of Sir Thomas More that we seem to find the Plato of the *Republic* redivivus. The *Utopia* has many references to the *Republic*; and, what is more, it advocates community of property and the emancipation of women. But whatever stimulus its author may have owed to the *Republic*, the *Utopia* is a different and independent treatise. While in Plato there is no little asceticism, in More there is something of Hedonism; while Plato had taught that society should let its useless members die, More suggests that those who are too old or too sick to get pleasure or profit from life should commit suicide. Penetrated by a different spirit from that of Plato, while borrowing, as he does, Platonic details, More is a typical representative of an age in which, "in opposition to Christian monasticism men lived like Epicurean philosophers, and in opposition to Christian scholasticism thought like disciples of Plato." When we turn to More's advocacy of communism, we come upon the same difference from Plato, which appears in his general outlook on life. The idea of communism may have come from Plato; its motives and its scheme are altogether different. The motives of Plato, as we have seen, are not economic, but political or rather moral: communism is necessary for the realization of justice, and because it alone will secure an unselfish and efficient government. The motives of More *are* economic: his communism is in direct reaction against contemporary economic conditions. Plato had felt that ignorant and selfish politicians were the ruin of the Greek city; More felt (as a Lord Chancellor said at the end of the fifteenth century), "this realm . . . falleth into decay from enclosures and the letting down of tenantries." He saw the agricultural class evicted from its holdings to make room for sheep pastures: he saw "sheep devouring men." He saw great landowners monopolizing the land, and men who would have been contented farmers betaking themselves to vagabondage and theft.

*From* The Political Thought of Plato and Aristotle (*London: Methuen & Co., Ltd., 1959*), *pp. 526–29. Reprinted by permission of the publisher.*

Agricultural communism was being advocated among the German peasantry by the movement called the *Bundschuh*; and to agricultural communism More turned. Since private property means such lack of "commodious living" for the mass of Englishmen, and since palliatives like equalization of property and inalienable lots are of no avail, let us go the whole way, to the final goal of common property.

More's motives are thus economic: they are motives suggested more by the evils of his own times, than by the reading of Plato. His scheme is altogether different from that of Plato. Plato's communism had only touched the two upper classes: More's communism touches every member of the State. Plato's communism had been arranged in such a way as to set the two upper classes free from all material work and material cares: More's communism is so planned, that every man must put his hand to the plough, and labor at husbandry. Plato's guardians had shared in common an annual rent in kind paid by the *tiers état*: More's citizens share in common the whole of the products of their country. Plato left the third class with private ownership of all property, and the guardians with common ownership of—nothing, except their barracks and their annual rent: More leaves his citizens with no private ownership, and common ownership of everything.[1] Of all these differences, the one which is cardinal is the difference in the attitude of the two thinkers to labor. Plato meant his communism— a communism consistent with private ownership of most things, and involving common ownership of very few things—to set his guardians free *from* labor: More meant his communism, which was real communism in all things, to set all men free *for* labor. In place of unemployed farmers tramping the English roads, he would have work for all: in place of the many drones who live in rich men's houses, he would have all men bees. In this way (all working, the lazy as well as the unemployed), he hoped to shorten the hours of labor, and to given all men a six hours' day.

It is obvious that More has many affinities with the modern socialism from which Plato so greatly differs. There are, indeed, differences between More and modern socialism. Modern socialism is generally collectivist, and believes in common ownership of the *means of production*: it is a community of *products* which More advocates. Modern socialism would not "purify" society of its "luxury"; it would only divide that luxury equally and impartially. More comes nearer to Plato in this respect; he would "simplify" economic life down to its elements of agriculture and a few necessary trades. But on the whole More has the spirit of modern socialism—he has something of its Hedonism, something of its zeal for a fairer distribution of this world's

---

[1] There is *no* gold in Utopia: in the *Republic* it is the guardians *alone* who have no gold.

goods, something of its close touch with actual contemporary economic conditions. And the problem of education is treated by him in the same modern spirit. Education had been to Plato the head and forefront of his scheme: communism had been, in comparison, secondary and subordinate. Communism is first and foremost in More, and education is considered chiefly on its technical side, and as meaning a training in some trades; for every citizen of Utopia must practice a trade as well as agriculture, and alternate regularly between the two— a suggestion which shows yet again More's modern and unplatonic view of labor.

In his attitude towards woman More is, in some respects, very like Plato. He believes in the emancipation of women: he believes that women are able to do the same work as men. As in the *Republic,* the women of Utopia bear offices: as in the *Republic,* they go to war. But it is not all who fight; and it is only the priestly offices which women can hold. Nor is there any community of wives: More believes in monogamy. There is perhaps something of Plato's physical point of view in the suggestion that bride and bridegroom should see one another nude before marriage, in order that they may know that they are fitted for matrimony; but that is the only approach towards Plato's attitude to the sexual question. There is no attempt to regulate population, except by the system of colonies, which Aristotle deprecates as a mere palliative.

It would thus appear that More, on the whole, is Platonic in the letter, and not in the spirit. He is rather "the father of modern Utopian socialism," than an imitator of Plato's communism. His aim is equality of enjoyment for all: it was the aim of Plato to secure perfection of knowledge for the few. In Plato intellectualism leads to the philosopher king and the rule of the all-wise Cæsar: More smiles at the idea of what the King of France would say to his Utopia. There is nothing of the ascetic despotism of the Idea in More: his motto is (as R. L. Stevenson wrote)—"Let cheerfulness abound with industry." Both in the *Republic* and in the *Utopia* there is some idea of religious reformation; but the difference is striking and suggestive. Plato would reform Greek mythology into a uniform conception of God: More advocates a quiet and happy toleration of all beliefs. *Quod credendum putaret, liberum cuique reliquit.*

## A. W. Reed: A City of Men

In his younger days, . . . More took special pleasure in developing themes of a paradoxical nature, which provided a keen exercise for

From *"Sir Thomas More,"* in The Social and Political Ideas of Some Great Thinkers of the Renaissance and the Reformation, *ed. F. J. C. Hearnshaw (London:*

his ingenuity; and at one time he had worked upon a dialogue in which he maintained Plato's principle of community in all things. Of this earlier experiment in Utopianism we know no more, but his seven months' sojourn in the Low Countries in the stimulating society of his scholarly and friendly hosts must, as it does with all of us when we are under the exciting influence of foreign experience, have awakened all that was keenest and most entertaining in him. That he should be called upon to explain to his friends his view of the state of things in England and to compare it with that which he saw around him is natural enough. And Erasmus is right in describing *Utopia* as an attempt to show whence spring the evils of states. If in his lectures on the *De Civitate Dei* he had distinguished, as St. Augustine does, the State or the city of men from the Church or the City of God, it was with the city of men, the State, that *Utopia* dealt. He therefore in nowise handles in it the wider conception of St. Augustine that ultimately and in every real sense the true State is the Church. That this was More's central position his whole life is a witness not less than his death. Like St. Augustine he felt the demand for absolute authority in a capricious world; the State must merge in the Church, the civil power become the weapon of the Church, legislator and magistrate be but sons of the Church, bound to carry out the Church's aims; the Empire must be the instrument and vassal of the Church. If this is a fair statement of the practical teaching of the *De Civitate Dei* it is none the less ultimately the principle for which More gave his life. With this higher conception More is not concerned in his *Utopia:* he is dealing only with the city of men. His *Utopia* is the criticism of the social and political life of the day, by the Hellenist standards of one who has the shrewd practical instinct of the reformer. He applies in a somewhat Lucianic manner the philosophy he had learnt from Plato and the ideas he had got from Plutarch to conditions and problems that he found at his door. But it is as a citizen of the city of men, and not as a citizen of the City of God, that he takes his stand. Therefore what More may say of religious toleration among the Utopians must be considered as having reference to such religion only as men by the light of their natural reason may enjoy. Impartiality would be a better name for it than toleration. Compulsion in matters of speculation would, of course, be unreasonable; nor, indeed, would it have been possible, had impartiality not been the rule of the Utopians, for Hythloday and his fellows to have taught the elements of Christianity to the Utopians. Subsequent history happens to have shown the State developing its control of the social

*George G. Harrap & Company, Limited, 1925; New York: Barnes & Noble, Inc., 1949; London: Dawson's of Pall Mall, 1949), pp. 137–40. Reprinted by permission of the publishers.*

organism, while the Church has virtually been disestablished; but in More's day, as in the days when our Litany took its present form, men could not think of false doctrine, heresy, and schism without coupling with them sedition, privy conspiracy, and rebellion, and attributing all of these evils to hardness of heart and contempt of God's word and commandment—or, as More perhaps would have said, contempt of "the Holy Church Universal." In the epitaph which More composed shortly before his death for his own tomb—his last retort to the heretics—he described himself as "not odious to the nobility nor unpleasant to the people, yet to thieves, murderers and heretics grievous." He saw in heresy a crime against social order, akin to theft and murder. It is no more reasonable to question More's consistency in this matter by the dramatic dialogue of his *Utopia* than it would be to criticize his attitude to the divorce of Henry VIII —the ultimate cause of his death—by referring to Hythloday's account of the easy terms on which the Utopians granted a separation. But I am at a loss to know how to think of those who derive any ideals of toleration from More's *Utopia*. Politically it was the most intolerant of despotisms. Even the colonists had to hold themselves ready to return home to adjust or stabilize the population. The individual must subordinate himself to the system. Nor did toleration—at first a modern political expedient—exist in the religious organization of Utopia. A man who did not believe in the immortality of the soul, in a future life with its rewards and punishments, or held that the world was the plaything of chance, was a man of base mind unfit to hold office in the State, who was not allowed to air his views in public. He degraded man below the brute; for there was a sect that held that even brutes had immortal souls of an inferior kind.

## *J. W. Allen:* The Saddest of Fairy Tales

. . . If the *Utopia* be a fairy tale, it is the saddest of fairy tales. More himself says that he had "taken great pains and labour in writing the matter." It was, obviously, so. The book amounts to an indictment of humanity almost as terrible as *Gulliver's Travels,* though wholly without Swift's savagery of resentment.

It is excessively difficult to get any change made, and yet everything needs to be changed. Among the nations of Christendom More's traveller cannot find "any sign or token of equity and justice." The rich men who control things

From A History of Political Thought in the Sixteenth Century *(London: Methuen & Co., Ltd., 1928, 1957), pp. 154–56. Reprinted by permission of the publisher.*

invent and devise all means and crafts, first how to keep safely, without fear of losing, that they have unjustly gathered together, and next how to hire and abuse the work and labour of the poor for as little money as may be. These devices, when the rich men have decreed to be kept and observed under colour of the commonalty, that is to say also of the poor people, then they be made laws.

\* \* \*

"The whole wealth of the body of the realm," declared an anonymous writer, "cometh out of the labours and works of the common people." More's thought was the same. Usurers become rich; but "labourers, carters, ironsmiths, carpenters and ploughmen," all those who do the necessary work "that without it no commonwealth were able to continue and endure one year," all these labor all their lives for a pittance, with nothing before them but an "indigent and beggarly old age."

For this injustice and absurdity there is, it is asserted, but one conceivable remedy. "Where possessions be private, where money beareth all the stroke, it is hard and almost impossible that there the weal public may justly be governed and prosperously flourish." For "where every man's goods be proper and peculiar to himself" and where every man "draweth and pluckketh to himself as much as he can," there will a few "divide among themselves all the whole riches" and "to the residue is left lack and poverty." So we reach the conclusion: "I do fully persuade myself, that no equal and just distribution of things can be made nor that perfect wealth shall ever be among men unless this propriety be exiled and banished. . . . Christ instituted among his all things common; and the same community doth yet remain amongst the rightest Christian companies." The evils resulting from private ownership may, indeed, be "somewhat eased" by law and regulation, but "that they may be perfectly cured . . . it is not to be hoped for, whiles every man is master of his own to himself."

All this is asserted by the mouth of More's imaginary traveller, not in immediate connection with the account of the isle which is Nowhere, but in the far more significant discussion that precedes that account. In his own person More makes the usual objections. "Men shall never there live wealthily where all things be common." Men are driven to work by hope of gain for themselves: under communistic conditions every one will idle. The dilemma is stated, but it is not resolved. It was hardly worth while attempting to resolve it; so obvious was it that the remedy proposed by the traveller, Hythloday, was impossible of application. To the doubts expressed by More, Hythloday can only answer that, if he knew the island of Nowhere, he would know better. Coming after all that has gone before, the answer is as sad as it is

witty. It was no answer at all; and it reveals at once the fallacy of
what follows. Proof of the assertions made in the first book of the
*Utopia* is supplied in the second by means of a picture of an imaginary
commonwealth, in which communism has actually resulted in all but
complete contentment, prosperity and stability. The picture, obviously,
is a mere assumption of what has to be proved. So conscious was More
of the fallacy that, when he came to describe his island of the blessed,
he let fancy loose and became little more than ingenious. He makes, it
is true, in the course of this account certain far-reaching suggestions;
but for the most part it seems to be calculated rather to amuse than
to suggest. It appears, too, after all, that this particular land of heart's
desire is not, on close acquaintance, so very attractive. "So must I
needs confess and grant," More concludes, "that many things be in
the Utopian weal public, which in our cities I may rather wish for
than hope after." Many things, perhaps; but surely not those houses
all alike, those people so much alike that they are content hardly to
differ in dress, that monotony of grave entertainment and garnishing
of the mind. But it did not matter. More knew that his Utopia was
nowhere and proved nothing. He had declared in effect that, men
being what they are, there is no conceivable remedy for social evils
except, at all events, one that cannot be adopted; and as to that one,
that it is doubtful what, in any case, the result of its adoption would
be. His book is the work of a skeptic in politics, though of a skeptic
whose mind rests in religious faith. The real land of More's heart's
desire was not of this world.

## *Ernst Cassirer:* Religion without Dogma

In sixteenth-century English culture . . . the religious atmosphere
of the Renaissance not only asserts itself, but presses forward ever more
triumphantly. Thomas More in his *Utopia* attempts to oppose to the
system of dogmatic theology an entirely new form of religion. He
outlines here the ideal of religion without dogma as the purest and
best worship of the divine being. More also revives Plato's doctrine
of Eros and Plotinus's doctrine of beauty. The cult of the beautiful
is not confined to intelligible beauty, to the νοητὸν κάλλος, but includes
especially the corporeal sense-world as well. Thomas More once said
that the right prayer to the Creator consisted in thanking Him for
putting the divinely beautiful human soul in such a divinely beautiful

*From* The Platonic Renaissance in England, *trans. James P. Pettegrove (Austin:
University of Texas Press, 1953), pp. 108–11. Reprinted by permission of the publisher.*

body. The religion and morals of the Utopians follow this rule. They represent a most decisive renunciation of any ascetic ideal. Even in religion, which elsewhere is nearly always gloomy and ascetic, the Utopians find authority for a way of thinking which by no means excludes enjoyment, but rather permits the greatest indulgence in it. For if true humanity, that is, virtue, which is the most distinctive characteristic of man, consists in alleviating the sufferings of others and in restoring joy to their lives; should not, then, everyone be allowed to apply the same maxim to himself? To be sure, not every pleasure agrees with true happiness, but the pure and morally good desire need never be shunned; indeed it may and should form the real goal of action. Hence the Utopians considered it simply insane to despise the charm of corporeal beauty, to impoverish the powers of the body, to turn agility into sluggishness, to weaken the constitution by fasting, to do violence to health, and otherwise to spurn the allurements of nature. When these things are not done for the sake of other and higher ends, for the welfare of society or the state, but purely for their own sake, the Utopians see in them an attitude inhuman towards oneself and most ungrateful towards nature. For nature is repelled by such renunciation, as if man were too proud to acknowledge any indebtedness to her. The eudemonist and hedonist ethics of Utopia has been considered as a remarkable contrast to the fundamental Platonic views to which in all other respects this work is so closely related. Yet this contrast is not so sharp as it at first appears. For, if one studies in detail the Utopian ethics, one finds that it is by no means oriented to Epicurus alone, but that it contains genuine Platonic thought. One is reminded, even in details, of the foundation and structure of the doctrine of the highest good as developed by Plato in the *Philebus*. This dialogue stands for the unconditional rejection of the pleasure-principle in so far as it lays claim to being the highest law of action. Plato opposes rational insight, φρόνησις, to pleasure— but he looks upon rational insight as the highest assurance of *"eudaimonia."* Not even corporeal desires stand necessarily as a contradiction and an obstacle to this ethical ideal; Plato marks off rather among such desires a sphere which is not only tolerated, but expressly acknowledged. Plato admits a pure pleasure, καθαρὰ ἡδονή, whose relative rights he considers as beyond dispute; this is the pleasure derived from beautiful colors and forms, also from scents and sounds. All these pleasures, like the pleasure of knowing, need never be excluded from the true and upright way of life. One should enjoy and retain them so long as they are valued according to their true worth, and subordinated to the fundamental norm of rational insight, φρόνησις. There can be no doubt that these discussions in the *Philebus* served More as a model, even in the details of the Utopian ethics. He by no

means defends pleasure as such; on the contrary, he is seeking a specific
norm of pleasure which will assign to each particular kind its relative
worth. In this pursuit he could also consider himself a Platonist in his
ethics; for he saw Plato again with Greek not Christian eyes. He saw
Plato not as an ascetic, but as a thinker facing actual situations and
as the champion of a new political and ethical reality.

## *J. Max Patrick and G. R. Negley:* A Definition of "Utopia"

It is questionable whether there are in the English language two
more ambiguous words than *utopia* and *utopian.* In both denotation
and connotation, these words have acquired a latitude of usage which
almost defies definition. The dictionary appropriately credits Sir
Thomas More with the coinage of the word, and then makes its cus-
tomary obeisance to the vagaries of usage by describing *utopia* as "an
impracticable scheme of social regeneration," *utopian* as "ideal" and
"chimerical," and a *utopian* as a "visionary," an "idealist," and even
an "optimist." Only the foolhardy would enter the lists against common usage; *utopian* has become, and will probably remain, one of
those verbal darts which the indiscriminate find useful to throw at
random in the hope of perchance hitting a target.

Quite contrary to this debasement in the vernacular, utopia represents in fact one of the noblest aspirations of man. What could be of
more significance in the history of civilization than that man, since
he first began to think and write, has continued ever to dream of a
better world, to speculate as to its possible nature, and to communi-
cate his longings to other men in the hope that the ideal might, at
least in part, become reality? True, there have been many utopias
constructed by crackpots, as many religions and systems of philosophy
have been. Some utopists have expressed as ideal what seems no ideal at
all, but in fact a regression from the real to a backward state. Others of
these dreamers have dreamed so vaguely or so ambitiously that what
they envision appears more like a prospect of heavenly existence than
any conceivable earthly state. Yet, in historical perspective it is clear
that the vision of one century is often the reality of the next or the next
after that; as the older ideal approaches closer to reality, the new ideal
extends its vision still farther. Utopia is eternal, and who can calculate
the inestimable influence which utopists have had in stimulating men
to the dream of a better world, of prodding them to reshape reality
closer to the ideal? In a few cases, we can point to rather clear instances

of influence which particular utopists have had in shaping the events of history, as in the cases of Harrington and Bellamy, to name but two. Generally, however, the influence of utopia is more subtle; sometimes the utopist accomplishes his end by indirection, portraying through his ideal the imperfection and inadequacy of the existing real.

The utopist, on the other hand, is not merely a reformer or satirist, not just a dreamer, nor yet only a theorist. Utopia is a distinct vehicle of expression, and it would be as meaningful to call "poet" anyone who scribbled a rhyme as to designate "utopist" any proponent of a scheme of social reform or change. Utopia is distinguishable from the other forms in which men have expressed their ideals, as philosophy is from poetry, or legal codes from political tracts. Just as one could hardly expect to appreciate the quality of poetry without realizing what distinguishes poetry from other forms of expression, so it is impossible to understand utopian literature if all manner of speculations, idealizations, vagaries, plans, political platforms and programs are to be considered utopias.

There are three characteristics which distinguish the utopia from other forms of literature or speculation:

1. It is fictional.
2. It describes a particular state or community.
3. Its theme is the political structure of that fictional state or community.

Any such definition may, of course, be considered highly arbitrary; but there are good and satisfactory reasons, both historical and analytical, for stating these three qualifications as necessary to constitute what can properly be called a *utopia*.

## J. D. Mackie: The Planner and the Planned-For

Both in his diagnosis of England's ills and in his proposed remedies More lays himself open to some criticism. The economic survey of contemporary England is faulty in several respects. The statement that women contribute nothing to productive industry is absurd, and of an age which followed a "domestic economy" it is more than usually absurd. Again, the denunciation of the men who raised rents takes no account of the rise in prices due to the development of the German silver-mines; the landlords, most of whose land was let out on fixed leases, suffered heavily from the increased cost of living and were bound to recoup themselves as they could. From a national standpoint

*From* The Earlier Tudors, 1485–1558, *Vol. VII of* The Oxford History of England *(Oxford: The Clarendon Press, 1952), 262–65. Reprinted by permission of the publisher.*

an increase in the wool-clip was desirable; some enclosure was justified, and the evidence seems to be that when *Utopia* was written the process of enclosure had not gone very far. The guilds were undoubtedly monopolistic, but on the other hand they could not be expected willingly to share with outsiders privileges which they had gained by their own effort at their own cost. None the less the fact remains that inside the guilds full privilege was vesting itself more and more in the wealthy and, in spite of the statistics, the evidence of Starkey and Crowley,[1] as well as of the statute-book, makes it clear that enclosure was already inflicting harm upon many helpless sufferers. The laborer, excluded from his holding in the country and debarred from employment in the town, was truly in evil case and worthy of the championship of More. Whether he would have really been happier in Utopia is a matter of doubt.

In spite of More's seeming reasonableness his ideal state was highly artificial; in spite of his liberalism, it was really a managed state whose people were not free. To bring it into existence the author had to postulate an extraordinarily fortunate geography, a fruitful island rich in minerals, surrounding a large navigable bay which could be entered only by one narrow channel; even the Robinsons of Swiss origin who "looked up and beheld the butter tree" had never such an island. He had to postulate, too, allies who never thought of repudiating their debts and the convenient Zapoletes who would fight as mercenaries without ever considering that it might be easier and simpler to take the Utopian gold by force of arms.

His planned state was a danger to world-peace—it resembled strangely the Germany of Hitler. It was an organized community wherein everyone had his place; where there was no unemployment; where the rough work was done by alien laborers or by the forced toil of persons who did not conform to the standards set by the state; where all citizens were trained to arms yet where few citizens lost their lives in wars which were conducted by "secret weapons," propaganda, and "fifth column"; where aggression was justified whenever *Lebensraum* was needed on the ground that an intelligent people could use land better than their uninstructed neighbors.

This ideal state was a danger also to its own people—as always the planner considered his own theories rather than the true benefit of the planned-for. For the ordinary individual, life in Utopia must have been intolerably dull; it seems probable that in the well-ordered feasts conversation must have languished and the food must often have been

---

[1] Thomas Starkey (?1499–1538) wrote *Dialogue between Pole and Lupset* (London: Early English Text Society, 1878) and attacked papal supremacy. Robert Crowley (?1518–1588) was a protestant reformer and a social reformer. See *The Way to Wealth* and other works (London: Early English Text Society, 1872).

cold. The fact that the citizens attended lectures before breakfast needs no comment. Life must also have been sterile; to what use could a man profitably turn his leisure if the capacities which he developed in himself could never be satisfied in action by individual enterprise?

Yet it remains a great thing that an Englishman had the courage to envisage a state which would be free of the social evils which afflicted the England of his day, and the genius to work out a system so complete in everything except in appreciation of the infinite variety of human personality. In designing his Utopia More was plainly influenced both by the old theories of the *Republic* and the *Timaeus* and by the new possibilities created by the great explorations. He lived in a world which was expanding in every direction and in which the fresh discoveries seemed to justify the wisdom of the ancients. In warfare, for example, the heavy masses of spears, developed as a counter to the charge of the men-at-arms, obviously recalled the Macedonian phalanx, and Aelian's *Tactica*, dedicated to the emperor Hadrian, became a text-book for the sixteenth-century soldier. Why should not Atlantis take on reality in some remote island? Yet there is evidence that More used authorities other than Plato and Vespucci. It seems likely that he had read of the travels of Marco Polo; the route adopted by Hythloday on his return to Europe is not unlike that taken by the bold Venetian; Amaurote in its plan and organization has some resemblance to the new-built city of Tai-du in Cathay, and the bridge over the Anyder recalls the wonderful bridge over the Pulisangan or Hoen-ho. More cannot have read *Il Principe* in print, for it was not published until 1532; but it was written, or at least begun, in 1513 and it must have circulated to some extent in manuscript, for it was plagiarized soon afterwards. In any case, *The Prince* was only a fixation—perhaps even a criticism—of the amoral doctrine of politics which was current in Italy at the beginning of the sixteenth century, and to these doctrines the *Utopia* was certainly a reply.

No doubt More had in his mind the *Praise of Folly*, which was a skit upon contemporary morals and manners; but he was an Englishman, whereas Erasmus was a cosmopolitan, and in the end it will be found that his main inspiration lay in the "condition of England." Obsessed by the social distress which he saw around him, he devised a country in which want should be unknown, and his approach to the ideal state, unlike that of Plato, was primarily economic. For that reason it is very much in tune with modern thought. One great scholar has pointed out that it is almost hedonistic. Another, arguing that Utopia represented the ideal of a people with the pagan virtues of wisdom, fortitude, temperance, and justice, but without the faith, hope, and charity of Christianity, concluded that "religion is the basis of all" and that the fantasy of More's early life is in complete accord with the spirit which made him a martyr for the Roman Catholic Church.[2] Certainly More was gay as well as pious in his youth and to the scaffold he took his gaiety as well as his piety; but it is hard to reconcile the liberal tone of *Utopia* with the austerities practised by More at various periods of his life and the tolerance of *Utopia* with the attitude towards heretics which he adopted in his later years. The truth seems to be that at one time More, like Erasmus, hoped to see a liberal reformation inside the old church, and that experience convinced both men that reform as it gathered force would tear down many things which seemed to them holy and precious. Confronted with a choice, they decided for the old and the known; Erasmus was deaf to the plea of Dürer: "Hear, thou knight of Christ! Ride forth by the side of the Lord; defend the truth, gain the martyr's crown!" More gained the martyr's crown, but not as a protestant.

[2] Contrast the view of Sir Ernest Barker in *The Political Thought of Plato and Aristotle* (London: Methuen & Co., Ltd., 1906; New York: Dover Publications, Inc., 1959) with that of R. W. Chambers in *Thomas More* (London: Jonathan Cape, Ltd., 1935; New York: Harcourt Brace & World, Inc., 1936).

## *E. E. Reynolds:* Reason without Revelation

Perhaps we now get misled by the very word "Utopia"; it meant no more at first than "Not-place" and had no greater significance than William Morris's "Nowhere"; but it has long become a synonym for the ideal state, and we assume that everything there is More's idea of perfection and not therefore to be criticized. This was not his view; at the end of the book, writing in his own character he said, "Many things came to my mind which seemed very absurd in the manners and laws of that people," and again, "though he [Hythloday] is a man of most undoubted learning and of great knowledge, yet I cannot agree with all that he said." This emphasizes the difficulty of deciding what More intended to be taken seriously and what he meant to be ironic or even facetious. The temptation is to dismiss as ironic or facetious those things we do not ourselves like, and that provides an easy way out of any perplexity; but there is surely a more satisfactory explanation. Let it be repeated that Utopia was a state guided by the unaided human reason; More followed this idea as far as he could, and showed us what the results might be of reason divorced from revelation. The striking fact is that his suggestions have in fact been realized. Modern society, with its indifference to revealed religion, regards a celibate priesthood as an oddity, it discusses proposals for permissive eutha-

*From* Saint Thomas More *(New York: P. J. Kenedy & Sons, 1954), pp. 92–93. Copyright © 1954 Burns & Oates, Ltd. Reprinted by permission of the publishers.*

nasia, and it makes divorce easier and easier. It is true that political assassination is still frowned upon, but "liquidation" connotes other horrors, and we all know the modern equivalent of the Utopians' "placards . . . set up secretly in the most prominent spots of the enemies' territory." Human reason can find convincing arguments for all these things.

\*     \*     \*

Much as one may admire some of the provisions of this imagined commonwealth, it is not, in fact, an attractive picture; the same can be said of other attempts to devise a perfect society whether by William Morris, or by H. G. Wells, or by Plato himself. They are all marked by over-regimentation and would be very dull countries in which to live. The value of these fantasies does not lie in their political viability, nor even in such attractive features as they may possess. They provoke thought on the problems of society. Plato's *Republic* stands apart in the strength of its influence on political thought, but More's *Utopia* takes a leading place in this form of writing. It is still the basis for commentaries and discussions; some are written with a ponderous gravity that would have made More "merry," though he would also have been startled at some of the ideas fathered upon him by those who fail to appreciate his mood and purpose. This continuing study of a book written in 1515 is a tribute to the genius of its author.

## *John Traugott:* The Alienated: Gulliver and Hythloday

. . . When Gulliver complains to his Cousin Sympson that some English Yahoos "are so bold as to think my book of travels a mere fiction out of my own brain, and have gone so far as to drop hints that the Houyhnhnms and Yahoos have no more existence than the inhabitants of Utopia," we smile with Swift the buffoon, but like More Swift played the fool only north-northwest, and dead ahead he means to say that the Houyhnhnms and Yahoos have the same sort of reality as the inhabitants of More's *Utopia*. For both *Utopia* and *Gulliver's Travels* are discoveries of the moral and spiritual reality of utopia in our everyday lives, and to this end employ as a satiric device a voyager who is maddened by a glimpse of the reality of the Good in a fantastic land and of the unreality of everyday life in real England. More's *Utopia* very possibly suggested to Swift that most essential and essen-

From "*A Voyage to Nowhere with Thomas More and Jonathan Swift:* Utopia and The Voyage to the Houyhnhnms," Sewanee Review, *LXIX (1961), 535–36. Copyright © 1961 by the University of the South. Reprinted by permission of the author and publisher.*

tially baffling of the satiric effects of *Gulliver's Travels*—Gulliver's utter alienation, his travels done, from the "Yahoo race" and his contempt for his "visionary scheme" of reforming it. And as both satires abandon their voyagers at the end in ridiculous postures of alienation, so they abandon the reader with the burden of bridging the ironic disjunction between the impossible truth, utopia, which cannot be ignored, and the shadowy actuality, England, which cannot be got rid of.

# Chronology of Important Dates

| Thomas More | The Age |
|---|---|

| | Thomas More | The Age |
|---|---|---|
| 1477 or 78 | February 5: Thomas More born | |
| 1483 | | Richard III crowned |
| 1485 | | Battle of Bosworth Field; Henry VII becomes king |
| 1487 | | Morton made chancellor |
| 1492 (?) | At Oxford | |
| 1496 | Enters Lincoln's Inn | |
| 1499 | Meets Erasmus | |
| 1505 | Marries Jane Colt | |
| 1507 | | Publication of the account of Vespucci's four voyages |
| 1509 | | Henry VIII crowned |
| 1510 | Under-Sheriff of London | |
| 1511 | Jane dies; marries Alice Middleton | |
| 1513 (?) | | Machiavelli writes *Il Principe* (printed in 1532) |
| 1515 | | Wolsey made Cardinal |
| 1515–16 | Embassy to Flanders; writes *Utopia* | |
| 1517 | | Luther puts forward the Wittenberg theses |
| 1517 | Enters the Royal Council | |
| 1519 | | Leonardo da Vinci dies |
| 1525 | | Tyndale publishes his translation of the *New Testament* |
| 1527 | | Rome sacked by the Imperial army |
| 1528 | Writes *Dialogue Concerning Heresies* | |

| | | |
|---|---|---|
| 1529 | Made Lord Chancellor (after Wolsey's fall) | |
| 1532 | Resigns as Chancellor | |
| 1532 | | Henry VIII divorces Catherine of Aragon |
| 1533 | | Henry VIII marries Anne Boleyn; he is excommunicated |
| 1534 | Arrested; sent to the Tower | |
| 1535 | July 6: Executed | |
| 1935 | Canonized | |

# Notes on the Editor and Contributors

WILLIAM NELSON (b. 1908), editor of this volume, is Professor of English at Columbia University. He is the author of *The Poetry of Edmund Spenser* and *John Skelton, Laureate* and editor of *Barclay's "Life of St. George"* and *A Fifteenth Century School Book.* He serves as Executive Director of the Renaissance Society of America.

J. W. ALLEN (1865–1945) was Professor of History at Bedford College, University of London, and the author of *English Political Thought, 1603–1660.*

RUSSELL AMES (b. 1912) was awarded the doctoral degree in History by Columbia University in 1949.

SIR ERNEST BARKER (1874–1960) was awarded decorations by many European nations for his scholarship in ancient and modern political history. Among his numerous publications are a translation of Aristotle's *Politics, Principles of Social and Political Theory,* and *Britain and the British People.*

DAVID M. BEVINGTON (b. 1931) is Professor of English Literature at the University of Chicago. He is the author of *From Mankind to Marlowe,* a study of late medieval and Renaissance drama.

ERNST CASSIRER (1874–1945) was a philosopher of the Kantian school. He taught at the University of Hamburg until 1933, and then at Oxford, Yale, and Columbia. His works include *The Philosophy of Symbolic Form, Myth of the State,* and many studies of Renaissance philosophy.

R. W. CHAMBERS (1874–1942) was Professor of English Literature at University College, London. He was interested principally in the literature of the Middle Ages and the Renaissance. Although his *Thomas More* is sometimes criticized as partisan, it is generally accepted as the standard biography.

H. W. DONNER (b. 1904) is Professor of English Language and Literature at the University of Uppsala, Sweden. He has edited the works of Thomas Lovell Beddoes and written a study of that poet.

T. S. DORSCH (b. 1911) is Professor of English at the University of Durham, England. He has edited *Julius Caesar* for the Arden edition of Shakespeare's works and has been principal editor of the bibliography, *The Year's Work in English Studies.*

J. H. HEXTER (b. 1910), Professor of History at Yale University, is a member of the Advisory Committee for the great Yale edition of More's works now in progress and editor (with Edward Surtz, S. J.) of the *Utopia* volume in that series.

KARL KAUTSKY (1854–1938), an influential and articulate Marxist theoretician and historian, was a dominant figure in the Second International and one of the founders of the Independent Social Democratic Party in Germany. His voluminous writings include studies of Marxism and an edition of German documents concerning the origins of World War I.

C. S. LEWIS (1898–1963) was Professor of Medieval and Renaissance Literature at the University of Cambridge. His writings include not only learned and brilliant works in the field of his professional interest but also spiritual autobiography, science fiction, and stories for children.

J. D. MACKIE (b. 1887) was Professor of Scottish History and Literature at the University of Glasgow until 1957 and has since 1958 held the title of H. M. Historiographer in Scotland. He has written on John Knox and on many other Scottish and Renaissance subjects.

G. R. NEGLEY (b. 1907) is Professor of Philosophy at Duke University. He is a student of political and legal philosophy.

J. MAX PATRICK (b. 1911) is Professor of English Literature at New York University. He has written on Bacon, Milton, and other seventeenth-century subjects.

A. W. REED (1873–1957) was Professor of English Language and Literature at King's College, University of London. Some of his valuable research on More and his circle of Friends is presented in his *Early Tudor Drama.*

E. E. REYNOLDS (b. 1894) has written a number of books on the subject of More. Among them are *The Trial of St. Thomas More, Thomas More and Erasmus,* and *Margaret Roper.*

GERHARD RITTER (1888–1967) was an eminent historian and political scientist and Professor of Modern History at the University of Freiburg, Germany. He wrote on Luther and on the German resistance movement during World War II.

EDWARD SURTZ, S. J. (b. 1909), Professor of English at Loyola University, is a member of the Advisory Committee for the Yale edition of More's works and co-editor of the *Utopia* volume in that series. He is the author of *The Praise of Wisdom: A Commentary on the Religious and Moral Problems and Backgrounds of More's "Utopia."*

JOHN TRAUGOTT (b. 1921) is Professor of English Literature at the University of California (Berkeley). He is interested in seventeenth- and eighteenth-century philosophy and literature.

# Selected Bibliography

## Text of Utopia

The standard scholarly edition of *Utopia* is that edited by Edward Surtz, S. J., and J. H. Hexter as Volume IV of the *Yale Edition of The Complete Works of St. Thomas More* (New Haven and London: Yale University Press, 1965). The volume includes the Latin text, a revised version of the English translation by G. C. Richards (first published in 1923), long introductory essays by the two editors, a bibliography, and an extensive body of notes. The edition of *Utopia* by J. H. Lupton (Oxford: The Clarendon Press, 1895) remains useful for its introduction and notes. The Latin text in this edition is accompanied by the first English translation of *Utopia*, that of Ralph Robynson (1551), more lively if less accurate than the Richards version. There are innumerable editions of *Utopia* in English alone in translations by Robynson, Gilbert Burnet, and others.

## Criticism of Utopia

In addition to the essays and books represented in this collection the following are suggested as contributions to the study of *Utopia*:

Adams, Robert P., *The Better Part of Valor: More, Erasmus, Colet, and Vives on Humanism, War, and Peace*. Seattle: University of Washington Press, 1962.

Allen, Peter R., *"Utopia* and European Humanism: the Function of the Prefatory Letters and Verses," *Studies in the Renaissance,* X (1963), 91–107.

Delcourt, Marie, "Le Pouvoir du Roi dans l'Utopie." In *Mélanges offerts à M. Abel Lefranc . . . par ses élèves et ses amis.* Paris: Librairie E. Droz, 1936, pp. 101–12.

Elliott, Robert C., "The Shape of Utopia," *ELH,* 1963, pp. 317–34.

Heiserman, A. R., "Satire in the *Utopia,*" *PMLA,* LXXVIII (1963) 163–74.

Liljegren, S. B., *Studies on the Origin and Early Tradition of English Utopian Fiction.* Uppsala: Lundequistska Bokhandeln, 1961.

Schoeck, R. J., "More, Plutarch, and King Agis: Spartan History and the Meaning of Utopia," *Philological Quarterly*, XXXV (1956), 366–75.

Surtz, Edward L., S. J., *The Praise of Wisdom*. Chicago: Loyola University Press, 1957.

## More Biography

*The Lyfe of Sir Thomas More* written by More's son-in-law William Roper about the year 1558 is referred to above, p. 1. There is an edition in the original spelling by E. V. Hitchcock (London: The Early English Text Society, 1935) and a modernized one by J. M. Cline (New York: The Swallow Press, 1950). The partisan but beautifully written biography by R. W. Chambers (London: Jonathan Cape, Ltd., 1935; New York: Harcourt Brace & World, Inc., 1936) is generally accepted as standard. *St. Thomas More* by E. E. Reynolds (London: Burns, Oates, & Washbourne, Ltd., 1953) provides some supplementary information. G. Marc'hadour's *L'Univers de Thomas More* (Paris: Vrin, 1963) lists year by year and in great detail events in the lives of More and his friends and occurrences of political and cultural importance in contemporary Europe.